HOPE, HURT, *and* HEALING

CATHERINE RENFRO

HOPE, HURT, *and* HEALING

Experiencing Jesus in the Wake of Suicide

B&H PUBLISHING®
BRENTWOOD, TENNESSEE

Published in the United States of America

979-8-3845-1373-5

Published by B&H Publishing Group
Brentwood, Tennessee

Dewey Decimal Classification: 155.9
Subject Heading: GRIEF / BEREAVEMENT / SUICIDE

Cover design and illustrations by Gearbox.
Cover image by Dave Waddell/stocksy.
Author photo by Gentry Parks.

1 2 3 4 5 6 • 28 27 26 25

This book is written for the glory of King Jesus.

This book has been his from the beginning and I am trusting him to do what only he can do in the life of each reader who is searching for hope in the midst of hurt.

Acknowledgments

To my husband, Chris—You have encouraged me along this journey of writing from the beginning and I am grateful. It's pure joy to serve Jesus alongside of you!

To my mom, dad, and sister—Losing Barrett is the hardest thing we have walked through, but you have stayed close to Jesus and helped others see how he takes what the enemy intends for harm and uses it for good. I'm thankful you were not only willing to share the journey with others through this book, but you encouraged me to finish writing it so that people can see there is hope in Jesus.

To my friends—Many of you have prayed for me, encouraged me, challenged me to finish writing this book, and cheered me on along the way. Thank you! Continue to pray that God uses this to do what only He can do in the life of each person who reads it.

To Lifeway and B&H Publishing Group—I am so grateful for the privilege of working with you on this project. I could have never dreamed of the opportunity, but I am so thankful that you have invested so much into publishing this book. Thank you!

Now to him who is able to do immeasurably more than all we ask or imagine, according to his power that is at work within us, to him be glory in the church and in Christ Jesus throughout all generations, for ever and ever! Amen. (Eph. 3:20–21)

Contents

Preface

One thing that too often holds us back is fear. Fear of failure. Fear of judgment. Fear of being hurt. Fear of _______________ (you fill in the blank).

As I type this, it's been fourteen years since my life was forever changed, thirteen years since the Lord began nudging me to write this, and twelve years of fear trying to keep me from doing so.

On October 5, 2008, my world turned upside down. Nearly two years later, during the summer of 2010, the Holy Spirit nudged my heart, urging me to write about it. "Write about it? How can I possibly do something like that?"

Some conversations with God you simply can't forget. This was one of them for me. I was on a bus ride home from volunteering on a student ministry trip in Orlando, Florida, when this conversation between me and Jesus took place. Knowing this kind of task was something much bigger than me, and not knowing what to do or where to begin, I took a deep breath, opened a notebook, and began jotting down notes. Several days later, I was sitting at home and opened my computer to begin typing what I thought would be chapter 1 of this so-called book. I hammered out less than a paragraph before the first wave of fear set in and I shut my computer.

What am I thinking? I asked myself. *I'm wasting my time.*

Within minutes, I had successfully downplayed Jesus's instruction to write and convinced myself I couldn't do it.

Fear of failure is real and debilitating.

As time went on, Jesus was faithful to continue prompting me to write, while I was persistent to keep saying no. One year passed, two years passed, and finally three years passed before I finally gave it another shot. Once again, I opened my computer and began typing, but it was too much. Reliving the events that ripped my heart apart and changed my life forever was too much.

Roughly seven hundred thousand people commit suicide each year. According to the World Health Organization, that's one every forty seconds.[1]

In 2020, "suicide was the second leading cause of death among individuals between the ages of 10 and 14 and 25 and 34, and the third leading cause of death among those between the ages of 15 and 24."[2]

Most people have either been affected by suicide or know someone who has, and yet it is rarely discussed.

Each person who has fallen victim to suicide has a different story, but they all have one thing in common: they leave behind family and friends who are completely devastated and full of questions. *How did this happen? How could I have prevented it? Why did God let this happen?*

The ripple effect of suicide leaves us frantically searching for help and hope. For me, the aftermath of my brother's suicide was like being in a sea of people and yet completely alone. Friends and family were close by for support, but the distance seemed insurmountable. I wrestled internally to grasp the reality that my brother, Barrett, was really gone. The nights were dark as I replayed every moment of that life-changing evening, and the days were heavy as my heart continuously felt overwhelmed with grief. I was desperate for even the slightest sense of relief.

Thankfully, there is light that can pierce our darkness and hope that can soothe our suffering. There is someone who meets us in the depths of despair and promises to carry us when we can't put one foot in front of the other. His name is Jesus.

After fourteen years of saying no to sharing the story of finding hope after a loved one's suicide, I came to the realization that Jesus's prompts for me to write this have nothing to do with me and everything to do with a message he has to share.

So the time has come.

Emotions resurface as I sit to write, and a portion of me once again wants to quit before I even begin. However, I know my story is not my story; this is God's story, and he intends for it to be shared. Paul says in 2 Corinthians 1:3–4: "Praise be to the God and Father of our Lord Jesus Christ, the Father of compassion and the God of all comfort, who comforts us in our troubles, so that we can comfort those in any trouble with the comfort we ourselves receive from God."

God comforts us so we can comfort others. It's amazing how God puts people in our life who have either walked in our shoes or are going to walk in our shoes, allowing us to stand in the gap for one another. I want this book to stand in that gap. My prayer is that many will read these pages and be assured of God's love for them, his nearness to them, and his faithfulness toward them in the wake of tragedy.

Loss is hard. Grief is complicated. And no one is exempt from the emotions, questions, and struggle that come along with it. Years have gone by, and I still find myself asking, "God, why did this have to happen?" But I can assure you, there is hope in the midst of hurt. There's peace in the midst of trouble. And joy comes in the morning.

> God comforts us so we can comfort us.

I've experienced it, and while the journey is not easy, you can too.

CHAPTER 1

Normal Life

It was supposed to be an incredible week. I was halfway through my first semester as a graduate student in seminary in Wake Forest, North Carolina, when fall break arrived. In high school, we did not get fall breaks. As an undergrad, I had two days of no classes, and now that I was in graduate school, I was getting a whole week off! The breaks kept getting better and better!

I had only one class on Fridays during my first semester of seminary, so as soon as class ended, I rushed to my apartment, packed my car with everything I could possibly need for a week, and drove four hours to visit family and friends in South Carolina. This is my home state where I was born, raised, and attended college. With only eight days to spare and several weeks' worth of things I wanted to do during my time away from school, I had to get moving.

I spent three hours and forty-five minutes driving on Interstate 85. When I finally approached exit 63, the excitement started to kick in. I was less than ten minutes from being home. I had not lived in the town of Moore, South

Carolina, right outside Spartanburg, since I graduated from high school four years earlier. However, going back during college breaks and now grad school had always been fun and memorable. I always stayed with my parents, who still live in the same house I was raised in. I paid a visit to Pizza Inn, where I waited tables throughout high school and during the summers of my college career, and visited friends I grew up with. There was a lot to look forward to in a short amount of time.

After spending several days visiting my family, my plan was to drive ninety minutes east to Columbia, South Carolina, to visit friends from college and then another ninety minutes to Charleston, South Carolina, to "rest" for the remainder of the week. A fun and relaxing week for me means running all over the place and never really slowing down.

This would soon change.

It was the second day of fall break, Saturday, October 4, 2008. I had plans to go to a Relay for Life event at the car manufacturing plant in Greenville, South Carolina. A friend's mom battled cancer off and on for thirteen years and was diagnosed with terminal cancer during my friend's senior year of high school. Her mom would share her story with the masses on this particular night at the Relay for Life event. A group of our friends wanted to be there to support her and celebrate life with her. So we did just that. She took the stage, and we grabbed a seat on the lawn. I will never forget the strength behind her words, sharing the journey she had been on for so long.

We ended the night with a once-in-a-lifetime opportunity. The car manufacturing plant opened the outdoor tracks where they test drive cars and anyone over the age of eighteen could drive the vehicles around the track. There were four of us in our group, so we split up into two cars. One car took the left track, the other took the right track, and off we went! We were racing to see who could make it around the track the fastest.

This was one of the most thrilling things I had done in a while. My prayer at the time was that we didn't wreck the cars because we had to "sign our life away," stating we would take full responsibility for any damages done to the vehicles. Thankfully, it was a ride to remember without any incidents.

I left the Relay for Life event that evening, not realizing that my time on the tracks would not be my only race of the night.

I remember the details like it was yesterday. I made it home just a few minutes before 11:00 p.m. and crashed for the night. Turning the sound off on my phone was a normal rhythm for me, and this night was no different. I put my phone on silent and laid it on the dresser beside my bed, and that was it; I was asleep.

At 2:22 a.m., my phone began to vibrate. Phone calls in the middle of the night are generally not good. However, it was not unusual for this particular person to call me at unusual times.

I picked up my phone, and his name appeared on the screen . . . *Barrett.*

Barrett is my brother. He was two years older, a foot taller than me, and between the two of us, he was the "cool" one.

Barrett was a great guy who had lots of friends. He was the life of the party and not someone you could just put in a box. My parents always said my older brother always got in trouble as a kindergartner for refusing to color inside the lines. His teacher would notify my mom and dad, but that did not stop him from coloring where and how he wanted to color. Barrett could not be forced to stay inside the lines as a preschooler, and he would never stay "inside the lines" as a teenager or young adult.

He was both stubborn and headstrong, but he had a Texas-sized heart. He would do anything for anybody.

When I was in middle school and Barrett in high school, he served in our local church and participated in mission trips. He loved to work and loved to serve others. Mission trips gave him the opportunity to do both.

From a family perspective, Barrett had a close, healthy relationship with each of us. We spent a lot of time around one another growing up. I wanted to be just like him. He played baseball, so I played softball. He kept his hair short, so I kept my hair short. But when he went through a phase of chewing tobacco, I did NOT follow suit; I had to draw the line somewhere.

Some of my favorite memories with Barrett involve playing sports together. Many Sunday afternoons, my dad, Barrett, and I would go to the baseball fields near our house after church to practice hitting and fielding baseballs and softballs. Sports were a large part of his life, and I joined him.

When Barrett was ten, my dad began a lawn care business so Barrett could learn what it meant to work hard, budget money, and grow in other life skills. When I was ten, I joined them in mowing lawns and laying mulch every Saturday morning. Once my younger sister, Kimberly, turned ten, guess what she did? She, too, joined in on what had become a hobby and part-time family business. While we often hung out with friends, most of our time was spent together as a family. Barrett loved each of us, and we certainly loved him.

My brother often put on a tough exterior, but he also had a soft side. He was a baseball player in high school and went to college in hopes of becoming a physical education teacher. He loved kids and loved teaching, especially if it involved sports. One weekend, he came home during his first and only entire semester of college and needed to rehearse a school project with me. He had to teach a "unique" lesson, and the lesson he chose was how to throw a Frisbee properly. Really? Does anyone actually care about proper Frisbee technique? I could not have been any less interested. Still, Barrett taught me the various throwing techniques and insisted I give it a shot. Being the nice sister that I was, I obliged him for the sake of his school project.

I say all of that to say Barrett was a good man. He was likable, caring, and fun. He knew how to have a good time, and he always kept things interesting. I looked up to him, as my older brother, so I tried to be just like him. The key word there is *tried*. Regardless of my attempts to be like Barrett, we could not have been more opposite. I was a rule follower; he was a rule bender. He tended to stay in trouble, and I did everything possible to avoid it. He disliked school and ultimately decided a college degree wasn't for him. I enjoyed school and continued on to complete my master's degree. Barrett usually stayed up all night while I preferred my sleep.

> I say all of that to say Barrett was a good man.

Barrett didn't care about my sleep preferences, though. I'm convinced that on multiple occasions, he intentionally waited until I was asleep to call so he could wake me up. That was my brother. That's also why the 2:22 a.m. phone call on October 5 did not phase me . . . at first.

Chapter 2

The Night That Wouldn't End

When I saw Barrett's name on the screen that night, I laid my phone back down to ignore the call, but an uneasy feeling rushed over me. I can't fully explain it, but I felt like the Lord prompted me to answer and answer quickly. So I did. I picked up the phone and pressed the button to answer the call.

"Hello?," I said.

On the other end of the phone, I heard a sheer panic in my brother's voice as he yelled my name repeatedly.

Some things can never be forgotten. Barrett's voice during this phone call is one of them. Even now, I recall the scream and the hopeless cry of my brother, and my heart races, and my chest feels as though it's closing all over again.

As my brother screamed my name, panic began to set inside my own heart.

"What's going on, Barrett?"

I remember asking this question multiple times before finally getting a reply.

He said, "Catherine, I can't keep doing this! I can't keep doing this to you guys!"

Completely confused and unsure of what he was referring to, I replied, "What do you mean?"

But Barrett just cried and cursed while repeating these words.

My brother wasn't much of a crier. I can probably count on one hand the number of times I had seen him cry. His tears alone were a sign that something was majorly wrong.

"Calm down, it's going to be okay," I said. "Everything is going to be okay! I promise!"

I had talked Barrett through some tough moments, but this time was different. I felt it deep down in my soul. Things were not okay, and I was unsure what to do or how to help.

I tried my best to console my older brother as he was drowning in a wave of grief, but nothing worked.

"Tell me what's going on!" I begged. "What happened tonight?"

In between sobs, my brother told me every detail of the night. He told me where he went, who he was with, and everything that happened.

Despite his past track record with drug and alcohol use, Barrett said he chose to go hang out at a bar. He said he and a friend got into an argument while they were there, and he began a long night of drinking. This was the beginning of the end.

As he recalled the night, he shifted back and forth between anger and shame. He was angry about the situation but disappointed in how he responded. The guilt of Barrett's decision once again to turn to alcohol led him down a path of what he thought had no return.

I vividly remember telling him that it was okay. He could go to sleep, sober up, and start fresh in the morning. But this was not enough. He kept saying he could not keep doing this to us and that he just wanted to end it all.

My heart sank when I heard, "*End it all.*"

This wasn't the first time my brother threatened to take his life when he was drunk or high, but this time, at 2:22 a.m. on October 5, 2008, was completely different. I can't explain it, but I could hear it in his voice and felt it in my spirit.

Despair can be one of the scariest places. It's a place that breeds hopelessness, loneliness, and lies. It's where the enemy, Satan, uses the weight of guilt and shame to lead us into believing there is no light at the end of the tunnel, that it is best to give up or give in. In Psalm 38:4, David says, "My guilt has overwhelmed me like a burden too heavy to bear."

The truth is, Satan will do anything to make us think we are stuck in a cycle we will never escape. Amid life's messy moments, he wants us to believe we have messed up too many times to be forgiven and encounter healing. He is looking for us to feel defeated. Jesus warns us that "the thief comes only to steal and kill and destroy" (John 10:10).

Despair can be one of the scariest places. It's a place that breeds hopelessness, loneliness, and lies.

The validity of this statement can be seen all the way back to the beginning when God created the first two humans, Adam and Eve. God gave them free rein in the garden they were living in and asked only one thing of them. He asked that they not eat from one particular tree in the garden, the tree of the knowledge of good and evil. In Genesis 3, Satan appeared to them in the form of a serpent and told them they would not die if they ate from the tree but that they would become like God, knowing good and evil. In this moment of deception Adam and Eve were fooled into believing Satan's lies. He convinced them to do the one thing God asked them not to do, and as a result of their disobedience, sin entered the world, brokenness occurred, and Adam and Eve hid from God in a place of shame and despair.

Thankfully, these lies from the enemy are just that, lies. There really is hope. Jesus goes on to say in John 10:10, "I have come that they may have life, and have it to the full."

Whatever our circumstances may be right now, there really is hope. We are never forgotten, not alone, and certainly not out of the reach of God's grace and mercy. Jesus says, "In this world you will have trouble. But take heart! I have overcome the world" (John 16:33).

CHAPTER 3

Racing Against the Clock

When Barrett said he would end it all, I pleaded with him like never before.

"No, Barrett, you don't have to do this! This isn't the answer! Please don't do this."

A few moments later, he said, "I'll call you back in a few minutes," and hung up. This was not what I wanted to hear. I needed him to stay on the phone with me.

In full panic mode, I immediately called him back.

No answer.

I quickly hit the "end" button on my phone and instantly hit "send" to try calling him again.

No answer.

I did this numerous times until he finally answered his phone.

"Barrett!" I yelled.

Crying uncontrollably, he said, "I'm so sorry, Catherine. I just took a whole bottle of pills. I have my gun, and I'm going to shoot myself."

"What?" I literally could not comprehend what he was telling me.

He's intoxicated and doesn't know what he's saying. I thought. *There's no way he just downed an entire bottle of pills that quickly. He wouldn't really do that.*

It was hard for me to believe this was actually happening.

"Barrett, I'm on my way over to your house now. Just hang on!" I begged. But he wasn't willing to wait for me.

"Don't come," he said. "You'll find me dead."

With those being his last words to me, the call ended.

Barrett hung up the phone on me a second time after telling me not to come to his house. Within seconds, I ran down the hallway of my parents' home and into their bedroom to let them know we had to get to Barrett's house quickly. As I gave a brief synopsis of what was going on, my mom immediately picked up the phone and tried to call him.

No answer.

She ended the call and immediately tried calling him again. No answer.

After dialing his number multiple times in a row to no avail, she received a call from him!

"Thank you, Lord!" I prayed silently.

Relieved that he called my mom, I remember thinking, *Surely, he's okay!*

About that time, I heard my mom shout, "You did what?!"

I knew then what had happened in the three seconds it took me to run down the hallway from my bedroom to my parents' room. Barrett shot himself, just as he said he was going to do.

To this day, it blows my mind that he was able to pick up his phone and call my sweet mom after pulling the trigger and wounding himself with a bullet that entered from underneath his chin, pierced his tongue, and exited from the top of his nose, but he did.

I tried to listen to their brief conversation while my dad jumped out of bed and put on clothes to leave the house.

My mom turned to my dad and said, "Barrett shot himself. You have to get over there now!"

My dad and I ran down the stairs, out the door to the garage, and jumped into his truck. From there, we raced over to Barrett's house.

As we drove along Interstate 85 heading south toward Greenville, South Carolina to Barrett's house, I sang the words of the song "Rescue," which was playing on the radio, over and over in my head but slightly changed the lyrics to reference my brother: "*He* needs you, Jesus, come to *his* rescue, where else can *he* go, there's no other name by which he is saved, won't you capture *him* with grace."

I was crying out to the Lord, begging him to physically rescue my brother and save his life.

It was only a twenty to twenty-five-minute drive from my parents' house to Barrett's, but I felt like we would never get there. There weren't many cars on the highway at this time of the morning, but we sped past every car we encountered. The situation became even more surreal when we finally arrived at his house.

There were cops everywhere, and an ambulance was already on the property.

I knew it was over but refused to believe it.

Maybe, just maybe, he survived the gunshot wound.

My dad firmly told me to stay in the truck as he got out and was met by an officer.

I was so angry that he did not want me to get out of the truck, but I tried my best to do as he said. I sat in the truck and watched in disbelief as the news was delivered to my dad.

My brother was gone.

There are moments in life that we cannot imagine, much less prepare for. This was one of those moments.

What are you supposed to do? What are you supposed to think? How are you supposed to respond? As someone whose life has been changed by Jesus and who has encountered the power and presence of the Holy Spirit on countless occasions, I knew deep down in my soul I wasn't alone, but I felt like I was in that moment.

I buried my head in my hands and sobbed.

"There is no way Barrett is gone! There is no way he is gone! There is no way . . ."

At this point, I don't know if I was talking to myself or screaming at God. All I know is that the life I knew was over.

The longer I tried to comprehend what was happening, the further my heart sank. I struggled to swallow. I felt as if I were being choked and punched in the stomach all at the same time.

I sat in the truck for what seemed an eternity. Minutes felt like hours. Not really knowing what to do as anxiety and pain gripped my heart, I picked up my phone and called one of my best friends, Margeaux.

The only words I could muster between tears and gasps for air were, *"He did it! Barrett did it!"*

Margeaux had no clue what I meant by "he did it." I gave no context to this statement, and she was rightfully confused by my call around 3:15 on a Sunday morning, awakening her from a deep sleep.

I then proceeded to explain that Barrett had shot himself and that I was sitting outside his house. Within seconds, she began praying for me and my family. There were no questions from her. No comments about the situation. She prayed to God, the only one who could help in those moments.

Having people in our lives that we can call at any hour of the day or night is nothing short of a gift from Jesus. Margeaux and I became friends in college, and she is undoubtedly one of these gifts. To this day, I am beyond grateful for friends who hold us up in prayer when we can't stand on our own.

In Exodus 17, a battle occurs between the Israelites and the Amalekites. Moses, Aaron, and Hur went to the top of a mountain, and as long as Moses's hands were raised in the air, the Israelites were winning the battle. If Moses put his hands down, then the Amalekites began to win.

If you have ever tried holding your hands up for any significant amount of time, then you know that after a while, the muscles begin to shake, and the body grows weary. Scripture says, "When Moses' hands grew tired, they took a stone and put it under him and he sat on it. Aaron and Hur held his hands up—one on one side, one on the other—so that his hands remained steady till sunset" (Exod. 17:12).

There are times when we need people who can come alongside us and hold our arms up when we grow tired in certain seasons of life.

As Margeaux prayed, my dad finally gave me permission to leave the truck. I told her I had to go but would call back later. I quickly hung up the phone, jumped out of the truck, and stood beside my dad. So many conversations were taking place around me, and my heart was filled with a hurt deeper than words can describe, along with blame, bitterness, and anger.

"How could this possibly be happening? Whose fault is this? God, where are you!?" I asked these same three questions over and over again.

You are no stranger to these types of questions. Things have happened or are potentially happening even now in your life, and you cannot help but question everything, including the presence of God.

Where is God in our darkest moments?

Where is he when you're barely holding on by a thread after a family member is diagnosed with terminal cancer, when a friend is killed in a car accident, when a spouse loses his or her job, when a child is living a life of rebellion, when a marriage is crumbling, or when someone we deeply love takes his or her life?

The answer is that God is right there. These words may seem too simple. I understand all too well that as accurate as they are, it is often hard to believe them in the heat of the moment. I felt a lot of different things in the early morning hours of October 5, 2008. But to be honest, the presence of God was certainly not one of them. That doesn't mean he wasn't there; I just struggled to realize he was there.

Psalm 139:7–10, says: "Where can I go from your Spirit? Where can I flee from your presence? If I go up to the heavens, you are there; if I make my bed in the depths, you are there. If I rise on the wings of the dawn, if I settle on the far side of the sea, even there your hand will guide me, your right hand will hold me fast."

This passage of Scripture encouraged me at times but more often frustrated me. Deep down, I knew it was true, but I struggled to align my heart and mind to the truth of this passage as I stood outside Barrett's house. I couldn't help but wonder, *If you were with my brother, God, why didn't you stop him from taking his own life? And if you are with me, God, why do I feel so alone?*

I used to feel a little guilty for questioning God, but over time, I learned that it's okay to ask him these questions. It's okay not to understand it all. It's okay to be transparent when talking to him. He prefers it! He already knows what we think and feel; we might as well be honest.

However, what we then do with these questions makes all the difference. We can either ask these questions and run from God in response, or we can ask these questions and lean into him as we seek his response.

While it may be difficult to recognize at times, according to what we read in Psalm 139, there is no place we can find ourselves, geographically or situationally, that God, too, is not there. He's omnipresent, meaning he is always in all places. This means God is by our side in the great moments of this life and our most challenging moments. Wherever we go and whatever we go through, he is there.

> You are not alone, no matter what comes your way. Jesus sees you. He hears you. And he will respond to you if you call out to him—questions and all.

Friend, let me assure you that you are not alone, no matter what comes your way. Jesus sees you. He hears you. And he will respond to you if you call out to him—questions and all. God says in Jeremiah 33:3, "Call to me and I will answer you."

Chapter 4

Troubled

Barrett passed away in the early morning of Sunday, October 5, 2008. It all seemed like a blur, but my dad and I eventually left the scene and drove home. It was probably best that we left when we did, but I was super frustrated because my dad and the police officers wouldn't let me go inside the house to see my brother. They were trying to protect me, but I wanted to see him. I begged them to go inside, but the answer was no.

When we arrived home, my mom and dad immediately turned around and left. They drove just under thirty minutes to my grandmother's house. G-mama is my mom's mom and one of my best friends in the world. This news was going to devastate her. My parents wanted to tell her about Barrett's death in person rather than calling and telling her over the phone.

Meanwhile, my younger sister, Kimberly, and I stayed home.

It was still the early morning hours, so Kimberly went to her room, and I went to mine as if we were going to rest.

Crawling into bed and pulling the covers over my head, I curled up in a ball and cried myself to sleep.

Just a couple of hours later, I woke up to a few close family friends sitting in our living room and visiting with my parents. Looking back, I am unsure why, but Kimberly and I decided to leave the house and attend church. I guess we just wanted to get out for a while, wanting to feel something normal. And since it was Sunday morning, going to church provided the only sense of normalcy we could think of on this incredibly abnormal morning.

I remember sitting through the service, unable to focus on anything. I'm not great at faking things, but this was one Sunday where I felt like I had no choice but to pretend everything was fine. Painful but fine. Although word was beginning to spread, few people knew what had happened, and the last thing I wanted to do was draw attention to the situation. So I sat there, fighting tears and appearing strong on the outside while crumbling on the inside.

As I look back at how I felt that Sunday morning, I can't help but think that most of us have become pros at living in a fake world. In a world where everything seems picture-perfect on the outside, we're hiding behind masks week after week. For some, this isn't just a Sunday morning church struggle but a daily battle. We attend school or work, and we act like everything is right in our world. We hang out with friends and hide behind selfies that we post on social media. Meanwhile, our world is a mess, our hearts are breaking, and we need help.

We all know life isn't always glamorous, but most people don't feel the freedom not to pretend that it is. I once heard a pastor say: "It's okay not to be okay; it's just not okay to stay that way." I had never heard someone say this, much less from the pulpit in a church. What an incredibly freeing statement in our culture where we feel pressured to always have it all together. In a world that's broken to its core, we all find ourselves, at times, not okay. And that's okay!

Having never heard a statement like this as a twenty-two-year-old, much less understanding that it's okay not to be okay, my sister and I slipped in and out of church that morning with tears flooding our hearts while forcing expressions of contentment on our faces.

We returned home to spend the next several days visiting with people who came to the house while also planning Barrett's funeral, which was going to take place three days later on Wednesday, October 8. My mom and dad, understandably so, didn't want to drag out the process, so they decided to have visitation and the funeral on the same day.

In a world that's broken to its core, we all find ourselves, at times, not okay. And that's okay!

Wednesday morning rolled around, and my family arrived at the church about an hour early. We were the first ones to get there, so we took an opportunity to look at my brother before guests began arriving.

Thoughts vary on open caskets, but I have a hard time looking at someone lying lifeless in a decorative box. Despite my preferences, I walked over and looked at Barrett. He looked "natural," so to speak, but seeing him hurt so badly. As I studied his face, I could vaguely see the gunshot wounds through the layers of makeup the morticians used on his face and neck. There were slight bruises on the bottom of his chin where the first bullet entered and on his nose where it exited. The wound from the second bullet, which we were told was the shot that took his life, could slightly be seen behind his right ear.

Seeing these marks made reality set in all the more. He really did this, and I don't understand how. I get even more frustrated to think that he could have survived after the first shot but somehow was able to pull the trigger a second time to end it all. How could this be? It didn't have to be this way.

After a few moments, we walked away from the casket, and friends started arriving for visitation. For the next two hours, we stood at the front of the church as people lined the walls of the sanctuary to speak to my family and offer condolences. This was a bittersweet time. On the one hand, seeing so many people who cared about my brother and had come from different places to love my family and offer support in such a difficult time was encouraging. Many of our friends drove long distances to show up, and the hugs they extended meant more than I can ever hope to explain.

On the other hand, questions like, "How are you doing?" drove me crazy as my heart was shattered into a million pieces. The outer expression of a head nod may have said, "We are okay." Still, everything inside me wanted to say, "How do you think I'm doing when my brother is lying behind me in a casket after taking his own life?"

These questions seemed a little ridiculous then, but I fully understand that people genuinely cared about us and didn't know what to say. To their credit, does anyone ever really know what to say in the midst of tragedy?

As the line finally dwindled down, we took one last look at Barrett, closed the casket, and sat down on the first row in the church sanctuary.

Moments like these feel surreal. Although we know it's actually happening, it's hard to believe it is real life. The only thing we could do was take a deep breath and pray for God's grace to get us through each dreadful moment ahead as the funeral began.

Often, we believe praying is the only thing we can do. It becomes our last resort when it should be our first priority. Prayer isn't all we can do, but it is the *most important* thing we can do. There is power in prayer as we approach God in conversation.

First John 5:14 says, "This is the confidence we have in approaching God: that *if* we ask anything according to his will, he hears us." We can come to him, our refuge and strength, and lay our hurts and needs before him.

The funeral service for Barrett was more of a celebration than I could have anticipated. Our former pastor, Roger, conducted the service and did what most pastors do at funerals: he talked about the life of the deceased—in this case, my brother. I think the one thing I appreciate the most is that he didn't sugarcoat the situation.

"Barrett was, at times, a troubled guy," my pastor said.

This statement could not have been more accurate. I mentioned earlier that Barrett couldn't *stay inside the lines*. He bent the rules and often played with fire. He didn't always make the wisest decisions and often found himself in situations that he should have never been in. Unfortunately, the last night of his life was one of these troubled times Pastor Roger was referring to, which led to all of us being gathered for his funeral.

Pastor Roger went on to talk about my brother, his passions, hobbies, gifts, and his memories of Barrett. The greatest memory he had of Barrett altered the tone of the entire service. Roger told the story of an evening he and his wife, Linda, came to our house for dinner.

My mom and dad took the three of us to church every Sunday morning for as long as I can remember. To be honest, we didn't enjoy going. In fact, I remember the three of us asking my mom and dad several times if we could skip "big church" and instead go straight to lunch at one of two restaurants, Kentucky Fried Chicken or Piccadilly. In case you have never experienced eating at Piccadilly, it was a cafeteria-style restaurant. Fancy eaters, right?

After years of attending church, my parents made a decision that would alter the course of our spiritual life. They decided that we, as a family, would visit a new church. The church we were a part of at the time was fantastic, but we lived just far enough away that we weren't involved except on Sunday mornings. Knowing the value of being plugged into a community of believers, my mom and dad took us to the church Roger pastored, which had a vibrant student ministry filled with friends with whom my siblings and I went to school. Within weeks, we were connected to the student pastor and a team of leaders who cared about us and intentionally invested time in us. We were also surrounded by friends with whom we began doing life. Our disinterest in church was transformed into a desire to never miss a time when the doors were open.

Just before Pastor Roger and Linda came to our house for dinner, we participated in our first mission trips with the student ministry. Barrett went to Puerto Rico with the high schoolers, and I went to Columbia, South Carolina, with the middle schoolers. As participants, we spent our days serving in the community and evenings together in worship services.

As I listened to various speakers each night and watched people engage in worship, I began noticing that they had something I didn't have. It was a relationship with Jesus, and I wanted to know more.

Roger and Linda came over to our house to talk with me, Barrett, and Kimberly about what it means to follow Christ. For the first time, all three of us understood that we were sinners needing a Savior. We also understood that God loves us so much that he sent his Son, Jesus, to pay the penalty for our sins so we could be forgiven for all we have done wrong and have a relationship with him.

The Bible says in 1 Corinthians 15:3–5 that "Christ died for our sins according to the Scriptures, that he was buried, that he was raised on the third day according to the Scriptures, and that he appeared to Cephas, and then to the Twelve." It also says in Romans 10:9, "If you declare with your mouth, 'Jesus is Lord,' and believe in your heart that God raised him from the dead, you will be saved."

That night, standing in the living room of our home, all three of us surrendered our lives to Jesus. In that moment, he became our Savior, our Lord, our everything!

Barrett's decision that evening to follow Jesus changed everything about the funeral service. Although we were wounded, we did not grieve like those who have no hope.

First Thessalonians 4:13–14 says, "Brothers and sisters, we do not want you to be uninformed about those who sleep in death, so that you do not grieve like the rest of mankind, who have no hope. For we believe that Jesus died and rose again, and so we believe that God will bring with Jesus those who have fallen asleep in him."

I took comfort in knowing that as of the early morning hours of October 5, 2008, my brother was hanging out in the presence of Jesus, not because of anything he had done but because of what Jesus had done for him. Paul implies in 2 Corinthians 5:8 that to be absent from the body is to be present with the Lord. Sure, our level of pain, hurt, and sadness was still off the charts. Still, we could celebrate knowing that Barrett was in a much better place because of the death, burial, and resurrection of Jesus and that this wasn't a final goodbye but simply a *see ya later*.

No matter how troubled one may be, this is the hope found in Jesus alone.

After Pastor Roger finished speaking, a friend of mine sang a few songs. The first song was called "Held" recorded by Natalie Grant.[3] The chorus to this song describes God's promise to be near to us when things in this life are taken from us.

Is there a song that floods your mind with memories? This is that song for me. When I hear this song, years later, I still crumble. It brings on a flood of memories and waves of hurt, so much so that I still can't help but turn it off when

I hear it playing on the radio. However, I can sincerely tell you that God was holding my family during the funeral on October 8, 2008, and for the days and months that followed as we walked the most challenging road of our lives.

A second song was sung, and before I knew it, the pallbearers stood, picked up my brother's casket, and carried him out of the church. We sat there weeping and watching as they exited the building. Minutes later, we were asked to stand and lead the way out the back doors of the church and to our cars to make our way to the cemetery.

The graveside service at the cemetery was short. We had a time of prayer; someone read a passage of Scripture, and then it was over. In a matter of moments, Barrett's body was lowered six feet into the ground. It was surreal. We sat there for a few moments, taking it all in, but rain began to fall when I stood up to leave. The timing was unbelievable. I remember watching and imagining the raindrops being tears from heaven as Barrett looked down on us, saw our grief, and wished things were different. Don't get me wrong, I do not actually think this was the case. Barrett was in the presence of Jesus with no care of this world, and there is no other place he would rather be. But the image still filled my mind.

Saying *goodbye* is never easy. Funerals are never fun. But I've learned over the years that pain and joy can coexist. You may read this statement and wonder how this is possible. I get it. Joy is not the first thing that comes to mind in the moments or seasons of life that are dark and painful. We will talk more extensively about this idea later in the book. Still, there is one reason why you can experience joy amid the pain. His name is Jesus. Loss of any kind leaves us heartbroken, but knowing what awaits those saved by faith in Jesus brings about a joy that cannot fully be explained. Revelation 21:4 says, "He will wipe every tear from their eyes. There will be no more death or mourning or crying or pain, for the old order of things has passed away."

Contemporary Christian recording artist Mandisa cowrote a song called "You Wouldn't Cry (Andrew's Song),"[4] which is written from the perspective of a person who has left this earth and entered heaven, a place promised to all believers. The song so beautifully acknowledges the pain that comes with loss, while so eloquently illustrating the perfection that is being experienced there. For months, I listened to this song on repeat, feeling like this is what my brother would say if he could speak to us from heaven. To this day, I still think this song articulates well what he and many others would say. If we could just see their faces, if we could be in that place, then we wouldn't cry for them today.

> Saying *goodbye* is never easy. Funerals are never fun. But I've learned over the years that pain and joy can coexist.

Driving home from the cemetery that day, I knew my brother was at home with Jesus, and he wouldn't want it any other way. But I still struggled to accept the fact that he was gone.

This is not how it was supposed to be. Or was it?

Chapter 5

But God

Suicide is a harsh reality to face. The mention of it alone throws our minds into a whirlwind of questions we may never answer.

How could anyone ever consider doing such a thing? What has to be going on in someone's mind to make him think this is the best solution? Does this person not care about anyone but himself? I hear these types of questions asked frequently. And while they are understandable, they oftentimes come from the perspective of one who is personally and emotionally removed from situations and/or individuals battling these vicious thoughts.

It's natural to want to pinpoint the *why* behind such a permanent decision, but it's not always possible.

> It's natural to want to pinpoint the *why* behind such a permanent decision, but it's not always possible.

No one mold fits all those who have either taken their own life or battled with the thoughts of doing so. Barrett is a perfect example of this. Never in a million years would I have guessed that one day we would find ourselves in a season of life where my own brother contemplated such a thing. There were no signs of it, no warnings for it, and in our minds, there was no real reason for it.

But God.

These two words are mentioned more than forty times together in Scripture, and they change everything because they offer hope that cannot be found anywhere else. In the Bible, we see example after example of everyday people who endured circumstances they wouldn't have guessed or even chosen, and in some cases outsiders made assumptions.

John 9 tells the story of a man who had been blind since birth. When Jesus's disciples encountered the man, they wondered why he was blind. "Rabbi, who sinned, this man or his parents, that he was born blind?" (v. 2).

Just two chapters later in John 11, a man named Lazarus was sick, and his sisters, Mary and Martha, sent word to Jesus in hopes that he would heal Lazarus. By the time Jesus finally arrived, Lazarus had already passed away and been buried for four days, according to John 11:17. Mary and Martha were devastated over the loss of their brother, and they wondered why this had happened.

But God.

He changed everything for the blind man as Jesus healed him by restoring his sight and for Mary and Martha as he raised Lazarus from the dead. At first glance, we might read these two stories in the Bible and think the miracle is the outcome of these circumstances, but there is so much more to it. There was a purpose behind the man being blind since birth and a purpose for Lazarus dying before Jesus physically went to him. In both circumstances, Jesus said these things happened "so that the works of God might be displayed in him" (John 9:3).

Here's a thought. Despite what some may say or assume, sometimes the circumstances in our life have nothing to do with us and everything to do with what Jesus wants to do in us and through us as God's work is on display. Maybe Jesus is using unexpected circumstances in your life right now to show you and others around you who he is, the power he has, and the hope he offers. That is what he began doing in my life after I lost Barrett.

Chapter 6

Asking Why

Fall break ended, and I had to return to school in Wake Forest, North Carolina. While time seems to stand still when tragedies happen, the world does not. At some point, we are expected to jump back into our rhythms and responsibilities.

While getting back into a routine is healthy, I could not have imagined ahead of time how difficult it would be. Each day had its challenges, but I quickly jumped back into my rhythms of attending class, studying, hanging out with friends, and working at the local YMCA as a site coordinator for their after-school program. Staying busy is a common coping mechanism. It was a way to temporarily keep my mind off Barrett, at least during the daytime. Nights, however, were a different story.

While time seems to stand still when tragedies happen, the world does not. At some point, we are expected to jump back into our rhythms and responsibilities.

When the day ends and things quiet around us, our minds race in many directions. Satan, our enemy, feeds on isolation. It's no wonder he waits until the still of the night to ramp up his game of attacking our thoughts. I remember lying in bed night after night with the lights off, tears streaming down my face, and my mind replaying, over and over again, the events of Barrett's final night on earth. From his hopeless phone call to the police officer's heartbreaking news, every word of every conversation ran through my mind. The weight of it all mounted, leaving me once again to experience more emotions than I knew how to process alone. Sadness spiraled into confusion, which turned to frustration, before moving on to anger toward God. Anger arose because God allowed my brother to take his own life, sadness set in because I desperately wanted to be near my family, and frustration festered as I began to regret following God's leading to attend grad school in North Carolina, where I was now four hours away from home.

In college, my goal was to become a news reporter. Still, the Lord had other plans and began calling me to full-time ministry. During my senior year, I began volunteering in the student ministry at my local church as a seventh-grade girls small group leader, and my world was rocked. Nothing was more exciting than serving with these girls and their families, sharing life with them, and pointing them to Jesus. God was calling me away from the news and into the ministry.

As graduation rolled around in May 2008, I had a decision to make. Just weeks before graduation, the student pastor, Nate, asked if we could meet to discuss a potential opportunity. Nate said, "I've been watching you over the last year, and I see a call on your life to serve in full-time ministry." I had been wrestling with this for quite a while. This was the first time the Lord used someone else to verbalize and affirm his calling on my life, which I had been internally contemplating.

Nate then proceeded to offer me a job as a summer intern with the student ministry. I couldn't believe it. I would get to do what I loved, but it was also a challenge because it was not a full-time job that I desperately needed. I was fully aware that the day I walked across the stage to receive my diploma and end my college career was the day I would begin inheriting all my bills.

Decision time came quickly. Would I walk through the door God had just opened, or would I pursue a full-time job as a news reporter at a news station in the state?

I knew what made sense logically, but I also knew what God was leading me to do. Often, these two things are different. With some hesitation but lots of excitement, I accepted the summer internship position at the church.

Funny how God always wins, right? Solomon was spot-on when he said, "In their hearts humans plan their course, but the LORD establishes their steps" (Prov. 16:9). You and I can make our own plans all day long. Still, God ultimately decides where we will go and what we will do.

That summer after graduation was beyond anything I could have ever imagined. My time was spent planning, organizing, and executing domestic and international mission trips, Wednesday night activities, and endless opportunities to pour into the most incredible group of students. The Lord confirmed his calling on my life to pursue a career in full-time ministry. As a result, Nate encouraged me to attend seminary and pursue my master's degree.

At the end of the summer, in August 2008, I packed up my life in Columbia, South Carolina, left it all behind, and began my journey of seminary in Wake Forest, North Carolina.

Fast-forward two months later, to October 2008, and I was now at a place where I questioned everything.

Why became the anthem of my song.

I regularly prayed, "God: Why am I really here? Why did I listen to you? Why did you let this happen? Why did Barrett go to a bar that night? Why didn't you rescue him? Why do you claim to be near the brokenhearted, and yet I feel like you are so far away, maybe even nonexistent."

I am thankful God can handle our questions and welcomes them. He allows us to come before him unhindered and fully transparent. Psalm 139 describes how he knows our thoughts even before we speak them. So, if he knows what we're feeling and thinking anyway, why would we hold back when speaking to him?

As the questions kept coming, so did an unnoticed sense of entitlement. This sounds strange, but unfortunately, it is true. I clearly remember praying, "Lord, I gave up everything to follow you! I gave up my own dreams to pursue your will for my life, and this is what you let happen? You allow my life to crumble! Why? How? I don't understand!"

Did you catch it? At some point, my heart shifted from an attitude of gratitude for the work Jesus was allowing me to be a part of in his church to a posture of believing he owed me something for giving up my dreams to follow his plan for my life.

Maybe you feel like you've surrendered everything to Jesus and have done all you can to walk with him, and yet you can't understand why life is not easier than it is. You may feel like Jesus should have stepped in and prevented something from happening the way it did. Maybe you feel like you've earned God's favor, you've done everything he's asked you to do, and as a result, life should look differently than it does.

This isn't intentional. Surely, we don't *really* believe God owes us anything. Friend, he gave us everything when he sent his Son, Jesus, to live the perfect life you and I can't live and to die the death we deserve on the cross so that we can be forgiven of our sins and adopted into his family as his children. God gave us his best by giving us Jesus, but it's easy for us to respond to trials in ways that say he owes us more, that he owes us an easy journey, that he owes us an explanation, or that he owes us understanding. And when this isn't the case, we quickly question him and turn from him.

For months, I battled the unrelenting weight of so much hurt, so many questions, and so many misguided expectations. We've all heard the phrase, "It gets easier with time." Maybe you have even been told this while walking through your circumstances that seem unbearable. Several people said this to me throughout my grieving process, but can I be honest with you? That isn't always the case. Sure, day-to-day life becomes more manageable. But even over a decade later, I can still feel hurt as though we lost Barrett yesterday and still wish things were different.

Wounds do heal, but scars can last a lifetime.

While time doesn't always make things easier, there is one person who can. His name is Jesus. Jesus, who loves you and cares about you more than you can ever imagine, says, "Come to me, all you who are weary and burdened, and I will give you rest. Take my yoke upon you and learn from me, for I am gentle and humble in heart, and you will find rest for your souls. For my yoke is easy and my burden is light" (Matt. 11:28–30).

Wounds do heal, but scars can last a lifetime.

The good news for all of us is that we don't have to carry the weight of our circumstances and questions alone. Jesus provides rest to the weary. He exudes light amid darkness. And he offers hope amid hurt.

This would become more and more evident to me as the days progressed.

CHAPTER 7

Lighten the Load

While I immediately jumped back into my classes after fall break to experience a sense of normalcy, the second class I attended reminded me that life was anything but *normal*. It was a biblical counseling class, and although I cannot remember exactly what we were discussing that day, I vividly remember the student who asked a question that crushed me.

As the professor talked, a guy sitting three rows in front of me slipped his hand up, and the professor proceeded to call on him. "Sir, you have a question?" the professor asked.

Without hesitation, he proceeded to speak, "Why do counselors tell family members who have a relative that commits suicide that their loved one is in heaven? We all know this is not the case, so what should we do? That's just a lie to the family."

Whoa! Really?, I thought.

My heart literally ached. A lump formed in my throat, and I could not swallow. Anger and hurt simultaneously filled every inch of my body, and pools began to well up in my eyes. I tried as hard as possible to fight back the tears, but it wasn't possible. They began streaming down my face.

I've got to get out of here, I thought.

I scanned the room to find the closest route to the exit. As soon as I identified the doors, I quietly closed my notebook, got out of my chair, and walked up an aisle that felt like a mile long in the auditorium-style classroom. With my head down and eyes fixed on the floor, I walked as quickly as possible while trying not to draw attention to myself.

I know this guy had no clue what had happened in my life just one week prior. But still, I couldn't fathom how someone could be so insensitive and so bold to present, as fact, something that is not biblical at all.

To this day, I cannot tell you how the professor responded or about the conversation that ensued due to his question. All I know is that salt was dumped into the open wounds of my heart, and I was ready to quit grad school and move back home.

I had no idea then that this was a commonly held belief. In fact, it was several years later before I heard this same question asked, this time directly to me, by a student. She said her parents taught her that suicide is an unpardonable sin, so she wanted to know if a person can go to heaven after taking his or her own life.

Having learned that many people will answer this question differently, we should look at what God's Word says for the truth. Not just when it comes to suicide, but his Word is the source of truth for any questions we may have.

The Bible says there is one unpardonable sin. While we will talk more about what happened to Barrett after he took his life, I can tell you now that this unpardonable sin has nothing to do with suicide and everything to do with rejecting Jesus and the gift of salvation he offers to us.

Shocked by my classmate's question and deeply hurt by it, I lashed out at God once again, "Where are you? Why did you bring me here!? Can I just go home now? Please!"

My phone began to ring as I walked to my car, struggling to hold it together. It was a friend and mentor from Columbia, South Carolina.

"Hello?" I answered. On the other end of the phone, I heard these words, "Hey, friend! I just wanted to call and see how you are holding up since going back to North Carolina."

Are you ever shocked at how things can just happen at the exact moments they need to happen? Someone reaches out to you at just the right time. A text message arrives at the moment you need it. Generosity is shown to you at just the right time. These "just the right time" moments are not mere coincidences; they directly result from God's work in the details of our lives. He sees, cares, and provides for us in ways that only he can.

Talk about a God moment in my life as I left my class in shambles. Even while doubting his presence, Jesus saw me where I was and knew exactly what I needed. Not only that, knowing my need for encouragement, he prompted my friend, who lived in another state, to call me at that exact moment. This is what King Jesus does. He knows what we need and is faithful to provide for that need at just the right time.

The Bible says in Galatians 6:2, "Carry each other's burdens, and in this way you will fulfill the law of Christ." I could tell you story after story about the friends Jesus put in my life that carried me through these long, dark days. Whether it was two in the afternoon or two in the morning, I never lacked people available to encourage me when I least expected it but needed it the most.

The easiest, yet hardest, thing to do is carry the weight of our struggles alone. I understand because I too often try to do it myself. Most of us have trained ourselves to smile and pretend everything is okay. Think about the number of times we greet one another, and the conversation goes like this:

"Hey, how are you?"

"I'm good! How are you?"

"I'm good!"

Meanwhile, one or both of us are wrestling with something that's crushing us on the inside. We have fooled ourselves into believing that we must appear as though we have it all together. As a result, we find ourselves in a lonely and desolate place, carrying what feels like the weight of the world on our shoulders.

You are not alone, and God doesn't intend for you to walk your journey in isolation. On multiple occasions, God, in his Word, promises that he will never leave us or forsake us. He also promises to provide for all our needs in Christ Jesus. These needs include people who care and want to help lighten our load.

In Luke 5, friends were lifesavers to someone they deeply cared about. The Scripture says this group of men literally carried their paralytic friend on a mat to where Jesus was teaching so that he could be healed. When they arrived at the house where Jesus was, the crowd was so large there was no way to get through to him. This wasn't going to stop them though. They were determined to get their friend to Jesus. So they carried him onto the roof of the house, lowered him down on his mat, and placed him right in front of Jesus.

Like the paralytic man in this story, we all have seasons of life when we need to be carried by friends into the presence of Jesus. Other times, we need to be those friends willing to do whatever it takes to get someone else to Jesus, including carrying them there.

> You are not alone, and God doesn't intend for you to walk your journey in isolation.

I am so grateful for that phone call I received moments after walking out of my counseling class. It was divine encouragement provided by Jesus, who is at work in all the details, despite our tendency to doubt him.

I fought the urge to quit school and returned to that counseling class two days later, but I could not get that student's question out of my mind. Does he really believe that everyone who commits suicide is in hell? Who taught him this? Where does he read this in the Bible?

I was so confident my brother had a relationship with Jesus. The Bible says, "If you declare with your mouth, 'Jesus is Lord,' and believe in your heart that God raised him from the dead, you will be saved" (Rom. 10:9). My brother did that. My brother had surrendered his life to Jesus. Sure, he still messed up at times and made mistakes that led to a series of unfortunate events the night he died, but that doesn't mean he lost his salvation!

"Or does it?" the enemy began to say.

Satan poses these questions and wants us to chew on them in isolation. The fact that the enemy uses isolation to attack our thoughts the way he does drives me crazy, but it's one of his most infamous tactics. If he can get into our thoughts, he can distract us from the truths of Scripture while making us feel we have to deal with them alone and defenseless.

Thankfully, we are not alone. We are not defenseless. When Jesus was tempted by Satan after being alone in the desert for forty days and forty nights with nothing to eat or drink, Scripture was his line of defense. When Satan said to Jesus, "If you are the Son of God, tell these stones to become bread," Jesus replied, "It is written: 'Man shall not live on bread alone, but on every word that comes from the mouth of God'" (Matt. 4:3–4). When Satan said, "If you are the Son of God, . . . throw yourself down. For it is written: 'He will command his angels concerning you, and they will lift you up in their hands, so that you will not strike your foot against a stone'" Jesus replied, "It is also written: 'Do not put the Lord your God to the test'" (4:6–7). And when Satan said, "All this I will give you, . . . if you will bow down and worship me," Jesus replied, "Away from me, Satan! For it is written: 'Worship the Lord your God, and serve him only'" (4:9–10). Jesus responded to every temptation by quoting Scripture, and the Bible says in Matthew 4:11, "Then the devil left him."

In moments where the enemy is doing his best to discourage us, distract us, or even destroy us, Jesus will use the truths of Scripture to guide our hearts and minds back to him. Sometimes this comes from our personal time reading the Bible and sometimes from a friend willing to carry the burdens with us and point us to the truths of Scripture.

Who has God put in your life that can point you to Jesus? Unashamedly, reach out to them. Be honest with them. Share what's happening and how you are feeling. Ask questions. Let them walk the journey *with* you.

CHAPTER 8

Distinguishing Truth from Lies

The weeks following Barrett's death felt like a roller coaster. There were amazingly great days and terribly hard ones. Candidly speaking, there were great hours in the morning that could easily be followed by miserable hours in the afternoon. Sometimes I would cling to Jesus and do my best to focus on the truth of his Word. Still, other times, I felt like I was wading through muddy waters, unable to distinguish truth from blatant lies.

More than once I found myself wrestling with my classmate's belief that suicide is an automatic ticket to hell. I knew in my heart this wasn't the case, but I struggled to figure out why he so firmly believed this to be true and if there was any legitimacy to it. After going back and forth in my mind, I finally decided to talk with my pastor in North Carolina.

When things are weighing on our minds, we have two options. We can ponder these thoughts on our own, often making us feel like a hamster running on a wheel and getting nowhere, or we can find someone to confide in for advice and understanding. The enemy would have us hide and struggle alone, but Jesus would say otherwise.

> "Carry each other's burdens, and in this way you will fulfill the law of Christ." (Gal. 6:2)

We need people we can confide in.

I waited until the service was over one Sunday morning and approached my pastor. The church was huge, and I knew he had no idea who I was, but I still asked if he and his wife had just a few minutes to talk. He was beyond gracious, and I sat down to speak with them. I explained to the two of them what happened to my brother, the question that was asked in my biblical counseling class, and the struggle I was suddenly having distinguishing biblical truth from the lies of Satan.

We need people we can confide in.

My pastor graciously began talking to me about spiritual warfare and how the guilt my brother felt that night is a perfect example of how it sometimes plays out.

Spiritual warfare is not something we put a lot of thought into; at least I had not. But it is a real battle in an unseen realm.

Think about it like this: in a football game, two teams are always on the field. At any given moment, one team plays offense while the other plays defense. For four quarters, there is a constant battle for the team on offense to get a touchdown while the opposing team fights to prevent their opponent from getting into the end zone.

Can you imagine watching a football game where only one team shows up to play? We know this would not happen, but there certainly wouldn't be a fight for victory if it did.

Just as athletes compete on the field, a spiritual battle is going on for our souls. Ephesians 6:12 reminds us, "Our struggle is not against flesh and blood, but against the rulers, against the authorities, against the powers of this dark world and against the spiritual forces of evil in the heavenly realms."

As Jesus and his team of angels fight for us, Satan and his team of demons are fighting against us. While Jesus coaches us in love, grace, and forgiveness, Satan is screaming lies of hate, shame, and rejection.

On October 5, 2008, at 2:22 in the morning, Barrett knew there was hope, grace, and forgiveness in Jesus. Still, the lies of the enemy led him to believe otherwise. Satan was screaming a message that he had messed up too many times, that he had hurt his family yet again by his decisions, and that there was no way he could, or should, go on living.

This is what Satan wants us to believe. He wants us to believe we are worthless, that we are failures, that we are too far gone to be wanted or rescued by Jesus. He wants us to believe we have no purpose, that we are unlovable, and that we cannot be forgiven. Maybe you've felt these things. Perhaps someone you deeply love has felt or is feeling these things.

Friend, this simply is not true. There is never a time when we are out of the reach of God.

Author Jerry Bridges wrote: "Your worst days are never so bad that you are beyond the reach of God's grace. And your best days are never so good that you are beyond the need of God's grace."[5]

We can never do anything to make God love us any less than he already does, and we can never do anything to make God love us any more than he already does. In a world constantly changing around us, Jesus is the same. His love for us remains solid and unconditional in our *worst* and *best* moments.

The enemy may have gotten the best of my brother that night and won the battle in Barrett's mind, but I can tell you that he did not win the war in his life.

> There is never a time when we are out of the reach of God.

My pastor shared Scripture with me from Romans 8:38–39, which says, "For I am convinced that neither death nor life, neither angels nor demons, neither the present nor future, nor any powers, neither height nor depth, nor anything else in all creation, will be able to separate us from the love of God that is in Christ Jesus our Lord."

What does this mean? It means that nothing can separate us from the love of God. Once we surrender our lives to Jesus, there is no mistake, fear, unwise decision, person, scheme, temptation, or *anything* that can separate us from God's love.

Just as I needed to hear this truth from Scripture, some of you reading the pages of this book need to listen to it as well. Jesus himself says, "I give them eternal life, and they shall never perish; no one will snatch them out of my hand" (John 10:28). Salvation is a precious gift that, once we receive it, can never be taken away from us.

My brother, Barrett, put his faith in Jesus, and because of that, his eternity was forever secured. Ephesians 1:13–14 says, "When you believed, you were marked in him with a seal, the promised Holy Spirit, who is a deposit guaranteeing our inheritance until the redemption of those who are God's possession—to the praise of his glory."

So, what happens to a person who takes his or her own life? While this is certainly not God's will for anyone, if a person has put his faith in Jesus for the forgiveness of sin, then he is saved. And anyone who is saved will spend eternity in the presence of God in heaven. Neither life nor death can separate us from the love of God in Christ Jesus.

After talking with my pastor, Jesus used Romans 8 to solidify my confidence that Barrett was with Jesus, and a peace set over me that I had not encountered in weeks.

What do you currently believe about God, yourself, or maybe even your circumstances that are contrary to the truth we see in Scripture? The enemy would have you drown in his lies of deception, but Jesus wants you to experience freedom in his truth.

Chapter 9

Taryn

I spent the remainder of my first year in seminary studying, learning, and, more than anything, seeking. I sought out who God is and what he wanted to do in my life. I was nine years into my relationship with Jesus at this point, and yet there were days when I had to go back to the basics of the gospel. I needed to be reminded of who he is and the promises he made. One friend acknowledged the importance of doing this and demonstrated it in the simplest yet life-changing way.

Taryn was a friend and leader in my church's college ministry. About seven months after Barrett took his life, she reached out to me and invited me to her house one day. I accepted her gracious invitation and am still thankful to this day that I did. It turns out that she, too, lost a family member to suicide. She had walked in my shoes and knew exactly what I was going through. She knew how I felt, the questions I battled, and the hurt I endured. She also knew what life looked like on the other end of the tunnel, having had years to process, learn, and heal.

This was new to me. Among all the people who played a role in praying for me and encouraging me along the way, not one had ever experienced the loss of a loved one by suicide, much less an immediate family member. Hearing someone say, "Me too," was a game changer. Satan wants us to feel isolated. He wants to make us think no one understands. He wants us to feel like we are in the wilderness alone. But this is not the case.

Taryn shared her story with me and began talking about Jesus being her rock during her most challenging days. I found myself leaning into her story. I wanted to know specifically how she kept going and made it through. Taryn said she had several "go-to" Bible verses that Jesus used to encourage her and strengthen her along the way.

Hebrews 4:12 says, "For the word of God is alive and active. Sharper than any double-edged sword, it penetrates even to dividing soul and spirit, joints and marrow."

A friend of mine says, "If you want to hear the voice of God, read the Word of God." This could not be truer. God's Word, the Bible, is as alive today as ever, and Jesus uses it to speak truth directly to our souls.

Taryn experienced the power of Scripture in her own life through the journey of grief, and what she did for me that day paved the way for me to persevere through the pain and later help others do the same. Before I left her house, Taryn handed me a stack of light pink Post-it notes. Knowing God's Word is sufficient, she had taken the time to write one verse of Scripture on each note for me to read and remember in moments when I was hurting.

I could spend hours writing out the numerous verses she gave me, but here are several that encouraged me and may do the same for you.

> The LORD is close to the brokenhearted
> and saves those who are crushed in spirit.
> (Ps. 34:18)

> Trust in the LORD with all your heart and lean not on your own understanding; in all your ways submit to him, and he will make your paths straight. (Prov. 3:5–6)

> The LORD lives! Praise be to my Rock! Exalted be God my Savior! (Ps. 18:46)

> Even though I walk through the darkest valley, I will fear no evil, for you are with me; your rod and your staff, they comfort me. (Ps. 23:4)

> Hear my voice when I call, LORD; be merciful to me and answer me. (Ps. 27:7)

> The LORD gives strength to his people;
> the LORD blesses his people with peace.
> (Ps. 29:11)

> We wait in hope for the LORD; he is our help and our shield. In him our hearts rejoice,

for we trust in his holy name. May your unfailing love be with us, LORD, even as we put our hope in you. (Ps. 33:20–22)

Your love, LORD, reaches to the heaven, your faithfulness to the skies. (Ps. 36:5)

Be still, and know that I am God. (Ps. 46:10)

Trust in him at all times, you people; pour out your hearts to him, for God is our refuge. (Ps. 62:8)

I lift my eyes to the mountains—where does my help come from? My help comes from the LORD, the Maker of heaven and earth. (Ps. 121:1–2)

He gives strength to the weary and increases the power of the weak. (Isa. 40:29)

So do not fear, for I am with you; do not be dismayed, for I am your God. I will strengthen you and help you; I will uphold you with my righteous right hand. (Isa. 41:10)

I have loved you with an everlasting love. (Jer. 31:3)

> He will never leave you nor forsake you. (Deut. 31:6)

> Do not be anxious about anything, but in every situation, by prayer and petition, with thanksgiving, present your requests to God. And the peace of God, which transcends all understanding, will guard your hearts and minds in Christ Jesus. (Phil. 4:6–7)

> Cast all your anxiety on him because he cares for you. (1 Pet. 5:7)

> In the morning, LORD, you hear my voice; in the morning I lay my requests before you and wait expectantly. (Ps. 5:3)

These passages of Scripture are constant reminders of God's love for us, compassion toward us, and provision in our lives. The psalmist could not have been more accurate when he said in Psalm 119:105, "Your word is a lamp for my feet, a light on my path." God's Word shines light on our darkness and gives us direction, encouragement, and strength when we feel we cannot put one foot in front of the other.

There were days I would take out these Post-it notes and read several verses at a time, filling my mind with the promises of God; other days I picked just one and tried to keep it with me all day long. In both scenarios, the Word kept me focused on Truth when Satan tried his hardest to discourage me with lies.

Taryn's willingness to share her story with me greatly impacted my life. I began learning a new level of dependence on Jesus and his Word.

God's Word tells us who God is. The Bible says:

God Is Our Creator

"In the beginning God created the heavens and the earth" (Gen. 1:1). These are the first ten words of Scripture stating who God is from the beginning. He is the Creator of everything: the heavens and the earth! The following two chapters of Genesis give us an account of creation as God powerfully and purposefully speaks everything into existence, including people. Imagine this: the same God who spoke the universe into existence, created us, knows us, and deeply cares for us. The Bible says in Psalm 139:13, "For you created my inmost being; you knit me together in my mother's womb." It is mind-blowing to know that God created us personally and purposefully.

Do you believe that? Despite all that has gone on or is going on in your life, God created you on purpose for a purpose.

God Is Sovereign over All Things

Lamentations 3:37 says, "Who can speak and have it happen if the Lord has not decreed it?"

To be sovereign over all things means to be in control of all things. Imagine this: nothing happens that doesn't first pass through the hands of God.

Maybe you read this and wonder. *If God is sovereign, why would he allow a person to commit suicide or allow any other hardship to happen the way it does?*

It is a great question, an understandable question. While we may not comprehend the whole picture on this side of heaven, we can know that the heart of God doesn't want these things to happen, but he allows them to happen because we live in a sin-filled, broken world. When Adam and Eve disobeyed God back in the garden of Eden, the relationship God intended to have with us was broken, but so was everything else, including the world we live in.

> Despite all that has gone on or is going on in your life, God created you on purpose for a purpose.

God controls all things, and while we will experience hard things on this earth, he isn't leaving us to fend for ourselves. In fact, we are reminded in Exodus 14:14 that "the LORD will fight for you; you need only to be still."

God Is Good

"The LORD is good to all; he has compassion on all he has made" (Ps. 145:9). From the beginning, God has been and will forever be good. The mistake we often make is equating God's goodness to a life of ease. That's not it. Good circumstances don't make our God good. Who God is makes him good. He is holy. He is gracious. He is merciful beyond measure and relentless in pursuing us. He is trustworthy. He is generous. And there's not an ounce of his being that doesn't want what's best for us. In every way he is still good.

God Is the Great Shepherd

David says in Psalm 23:1–3, "The LORD is my shepherd, I lack nothing. He makes me lie down in green pastures, he leads me beside quiet waters, he refreshes my soul." The image David paints here is a calming portrait of who God is as the Great Shepherd and what he does for us as his sheep. Before David was a king, he spent time hiding out in the desert; he was a shepherd. This is one of the reasons he could write Psalm 23 from the lens of a sheep.

Having been a shepherd and hidden in the desert for so long, he knew what it meant to be desperate for God. Think for a moment about sheep in the desert. They would have minimal food, minimal water, and minimal protection. Without someone to protect and provide for them, sheep would be vulnerable to starvation, thirst, and predator attacks.

In the same way, apart from the Great Shepherd, we, too, are vulnerable to everything including discouragement, loss of joy, pride, burnout, and sin. As we come into his care through faith in Jesus, he protects us, provides for us, and restores our souls.

God Is Light

Psalm 27:1 says, "The LORD is my light and my salvation—whom shall I fear? The LORD is the stronghold of my life—of whom shall I be afraid?" Light shining into darkness looks like hope in the midst of hurt, peace in the presence of pain, freedom overcoming shame, forgiveness in place of sin, and new beginnings as Jesus transforms our hearts and minds. God is the light we long for when the path ahead seems dim.

These are just a few of many descriptors of who God is. Take some time to dive into the Scriptures for yourself, and you'll discover more of who he is. You will also uncover his promises to you and me, giving us hope for today and eternity.

> Apart from the Great Shepherd, we, too, are vulnerable to everything including discouragement, loss of joy, pride, burnout, and sin.

What does God promise?

He promises never to leave or abandon us.

> Have I not commanded you? Be strong and courageous. Do not be afraid; do not be discouraged, for the LORD your God will be with you wherever you go. (Josh. 1:9)

> Never will I leave you; never will I forsake you. (Heb. 13:5)

He promises rest.

> Come to me, all you who are weary and burdened, and I will give you rest. (Matt. 11:28)

He promises unfailing love.

> I have loved you with an everlasting love. (Jer. 31:3)

He promises that we will find him when we search for him.

> You will seek me and find me when you seek me with all your heart. (Jer. 29:13)

He promises to provide for us.

> And my God will meet all your needs according to the riches of his glory in Christ Jesus. (Phil. 4:19)

He promises hope.

> "For I know the plans I have for you," declares the LORD, "plans to prosper you and not to harm you, plans to give you a hope and a future." (Jer. 29:11)

God has done countless things throughout all of history, but one thing he has never done is break a promise. In Psalm 89:34, God says, "I will not violate my covenant or alter what my lips have uttered." We can trust him as we hold tightly to his promises.

I often wish my brother had clung as tightly to these promises the night he took his life as I have found myself doing each day following his death. He knew these promises. In fact, these same promises kept Barrett going on several other occasions. I was a junior in college the first time he threatened to take his life. He called me well into the night and was hysterical. In a similar situation to his last night on earth, he had been drinking heavily that evening. Something happened unbeknown to me, and he felt like a failure and a disappointment to those who loved him most. The lies filling his mind led him to believe he would be better off dead and that we would be better off if he were dead.

I type these words and still get frustrated and hurt today. How can someone believe this to be true? How could Barrett believe this was true? A part of me wants to scream out, "It's not true! It's a lie from hell! Satan wants you to believe this! It's not true; just stop thinking that!" These thoughts imply there is a switch someone can turn off and on in their mind. Unfortunately, it is just not that simple. Barrett taught me that.

Sure, some of his thoughts stemmed from his altered state of mind after having too much to drink or after using various substances. Still, these thoughts often lingered in the back of his mind as he regretted setbacks and relapses.

Barrett felt defeated, just as so many people do today. But God's promises gave him the strength to press on when I was in college—the promise of forgiveness, God's faithfulness, and grace.

Some have asked if the promises of God weren't enough the night Barrett decided to take his life and end it all. It's a fair question, but knowing what I know now, I'm confident that Barrett, in his last moments, held tightly to the assurance found in 2 Corinthians 5, which shows us that to be absent from the body is to be present with the Lord. Barrett was tired of the battle. And while he was mistaken to think we would be better off without him, he was correct in that he would leave this earth and go to a much better place: his eternal home in heaven with Jesus.

Barrett's decision to take matters into his own hands on October 5, 2008, certainly didn't make it easy for our family. Still, God kindly allowed us to hold his hand in the days ahead. I'm particularly grateful for the morning when the Lord began putting things into perspective for me.

It was a Sunday morning. I awoke to the sound of my alarm and went to church. I was by myself that Sunday, which was a God thing. The message was about trusting God and could not have been more timely. Have you ever sat through a sermon, message, or speech and thought the person was talking directly to you? That is how I felt that Sunday.

My pastor preached from the book of Exodus, and I left church that morning not only encouraged but beginning to process and see the "wilderness" in a new light. I began to see it in light of God's promises.

In the book of Exodus, we read about God leading his people through the wilderness for forty years while having a specific plan and purpose in mind.

In Exodus 3, God gave Moses a command to rescue the Israelites from a life of slavery in Egypt and to lead them to the promised land. Moses, feeling completely inadequate, replied, "Who am I that I should go to Pharaoh and bring the Israelites out of Egypt?" (v. 11). Despite God's assuring Moses that he would be with him and giving Moses instructions on what to say and do, Moses was reluctant to go to Egypt. "What if they do not believe me or listen to me and say, 'The LORD did not appear to you'?" (Exod. 4:1).

Moses said to the LORD, "Pardon your servant, Lord. I have never been eloquent, neither in the past nor since you have spoken to your servant. I am slow of speech and tongue" (Exod. 4:10).

The LORD said to him, "Who gave human beings their mouths? Who makes them deaf or mute? Who gives them sight or makes them blind? Is it not I, the LORD? Now go; I will help you speak and will teach you what to say" (Exod. 4:11–12).

By this time, Moses appears to be out of excuses, and he went to Egypt as God instructed him to do. The task before him wasn't easy, but after many back-and-forth conversations with Pharaoh in Egypt and plagues sent by God to the Egyptian people, Moses did what God sent him to do. He led the Israelites, who had been enslaved for four hundred years, out of Egypt.

At this point, the plan of getting the Israelites out of Egypt and to the promised land was in full swing. Moses knew what he had to do, where they were going, and the purpose behind what they were doing.

It sounds like a great win. The Israelites were no longer in slavery, and they were on their way to a life of complete freedom.

Just as life throws you and me curveballs, the same thing happened with Moses and the Israelites. After leaving

Egypt, they endured circumstances they never dreamed of. They found themselves wandering through the wilderness, a literal desert, for forty years, facing many difficulties and upsets.

At one point, they were in the dry, hot desert without water and complained profusely to Moses. Another time, they were without food to eat, and not only did they complain, but unable to see what was ahead, they wished they were back in Egypt. Their exact words were, "If only we had died by the LORD's hand in Egypt! There we sat around pots of meat and ate all the food we wanted, but you have brought us out into this desert to starve this entire assembly to death" (Exod. 16:3).

Although Moses tried to encourage the Israelites and point them toward God and his faithfulness, they were so frustrated by their circumstances that they genuinely believed they were better off back in Egypt, where they were kept as slaves. Can you imagine being in such difficult circumstances that being enslaved sounds more appealing?

The phrase, "You can't see the forest through the trees," is all too familiar when we, like the Israelites, walk along some of life's rockiest paths. Our immediate circumstances can block our vision and prevent us from seeing the bigger picture.

I can't tell you how many times I heard people say the following phrases after Barrett passed away:

"Catherine, God has a plan; just trust him."

"Hang in there, God will provide."

"Hey friend, God is going to use this for good."

"God is still in control."

Each of these statements was intended to be words of encouragement. Yes, our hearts absolutely need to hear these truths, but I'll be the first to say that they can be hard to hear, much less comprehend, when you are in the wilderness.

I knew these things to be true; I really believed them to be true, but it was hard to see how God could possibly be at work. I couldn't, at the time, grasp how God could ever use Barrett's death for good. And I certainly questioned God's position of control. The bigger picture was being blocked by obstacles of raw emotions and lies from the enemy.

Thankfully, the forest was still intact, and God was at work for my good and his glory, just as he promised.

If you continue walking through the book of Exodus, you read that each time the Israelites were in need, God showed up and provided in a way only he could do. He provided water when they were thirsty, manna when they were hungry, and guidance when they were lost. All the while, he was testing them and teaching them. The Bible says in Deuteronomy 8:2–3: "Remember how the LORD your God led you all the way in the wilderness these forty years, to humble and test you in order to know what was in your heart, whether or not you would keep his commands. He humbled you, causing you to hunger and then feeding you with manna, which neither you nor your ancestors had known, to teach you that man does not live on bread alone but on every word that comes from the mouth of the Lord."

God wanted the Israelites to see their need to depend on him. He also wanted them to see that he is faithful to provide.

Just as God had a plan for the Israelites who were venturing through the wilderness for forty years, he has a plan for our lives today. Though there are times when we feel *lost*, we can keep taking steps forward in confidence, knowing God will lead us and teach us along the way, just as he has promised.

Though there are times when we feel *lost*, we can keep taking steps forward in confidence, knowing God will lead us and teach us along the way, just as he has promised.

Today, you can know that God is with you. He will provide for you. He loves you. He is for you. And you can trust him. Hold onto his promises, even when life hurts. Write them on a Post-it note as a reminder and keep going.

CHAPTER 10

A Glimmer of Hope

Most people tend to do one of two things when hard things happen. We either shut down and isolate ourselves or try to keep ourselves busy. Which do you do most often? There's no right or wrong way to answer this question. We're all different, and we respond to things differently. It's no secret that I keep myself preoccupied with as much normalcy as possible. Whether good or bad, staying busy is a means to keep my mind off the difficult situations at hand.

With that being said, my decision to drive from Wake Forest, North Carolina, back to Columbia, South Carolina, on Thursday, November 15, 2008, a mere thirty-four days after Barrett's death, to serve during a fall retreat weekend was not out of the norm. I loved serving and would never turn down an opportunity to serve the students in my home church's ministry.

On the morning of Friday, November 16, I showed up at the church bright and early to meet with a friend, the interim student minister at the time. As we discussed the upcoming weekend, he caught me off guard with two questions.

First, he asked if he could mention my brother's story in one of his messages over the weekend. This question doesn't seem like that big of a deal, but it was all so fresh that even the mention of Barrett's name still shattered me. I wasn't sure if I was ready for that.

Second, he asked if I would be willing to share during the Sunday morning session to wrap up the retreat weekend.

I remember saying "Yes, of course!" to both questions, but I also remember thinking, *What have I gotten myself into? This is going to be rough.*

Sometimes my optimism can outweigh my realism, so I can easily say yes to something before putting the appropriate amount of thought or prayer into it. I love opportunities to point people to Jesus, but I didn't really feel like I could do so while Barrett's death was so recent and my pain so fresh.

Around noon that day, I took a lunch break and took the time to think through the weekend. What would the Lord have me do? While thinking, praying, and talking with a friend, doubt began flooding my mind, and my thoughts ran rampant:

> *"The mention of my brother's story is too much to bear right now."*
>
> *"How can I speak during such a raw season?"*
>
> *"I should have said no."*

As these thoughts persisted, I paused, took a deep breath, and prayed. The Lord was my only answer; he would have to give me the strength, courage, and words to say if I was going to move forward.

I finished lunch and returned to the church to help pack supplies and prepare to leave.

Around 5:00 that evening, 120 students began pouring into the church. I had not seen them since going to seminary. I loved being back and catching up with them.

Despite the excitement of reuniting with these students and their families, I began to feel an overwhelming sense of anxiety. A few people mentioned my brother and asked about my family, which brought many emotions. The combination of these conversations, the chaos of getting everyone settled so we could leave for the retreat, and pondering the fact that I had committed to speaking put me on edge. Anxiety and adrenaline were getting the best of me.

Eventually, we loaded the buses, closed the doors, and were on our way. As we pulled onto the highway, a glimpse of reality set in, and I began missing Barrett terribly. Tears fell down my cheeks, and I was so thankful I was driving one of the buses because no one could see my face. My heart was hurting, and once again, all I could think was, *He is really gone*.

It is interesting how these waves of pain can rush in without warning. I have since learned that after experiencing a tragedy, it's normal to feel fine one minute and fall apart the next. I'll be honest, though; it made me feel like I was crazy. How does one move from talking and laughing one moment to tears and aching the next? I don't know how, but it happens. And it's okay.

The first forty-five minutes of the bus drive were miserable, and I wondered why I was going. I had nothing to offer during this fall retreat weekend; at least, that's what I had convinced myself to believe.

Once again, all I could do was pray. While writing this book, I found these words written in my journal from that particular night:

> *Father, I feel like an emotional wreck. I'm hurting so much and can't begin to explain how it feels. I'm not sure why I came. I can already tell this weekend is going to be tough . . . but take control. I'm praying for salvation to occur this weekend. I know people are hurting on this trip just as much as I am right now. Students are facing situations that are just as difficult and painful as mine. Pour out your Spirit on all of us this weekend and change us! For those who don't know you as Savior, capture their hearts this weekend. Father, use me. As I prepare for Sunday morning, give me the words to say to these students. I love you, Lord.*
>
> *Your Daughter,*
>
> *Catherine*

These words are raw, but I'm glad I wrote them down. Journaling is a simple way to unleash our thoughts and prayers while also documenting where we are so that months, maybe even years, down the road, we can see where

God brought us from and be reminded all over again of his faithfulness on display.

The Israelites in the Old Testament of the Bible did something similar. Maybe they didn't journal, but they did lay down stones of remembrance. In Joshua 4, the Israelites were told to cross the Jordan River. The only problem is that the Jordan River was flooded. When the priests carrying the ark of the Lord came to the river, God caused the waters from upstream to stop flowing so that the Israelites could cross over the Jordan. Then Joshua called the people together and told them to gather twelve huge stones to serve as a sign among them. He said, "In the future, when your children ask you, 'What do these stones mean?' tell them that the flow of the Jordan was cut off before the ark of the covenant of the LORD. When it crossed the Jordan, the waters of the Jordan were cut off. These stones are to be a memorial to the people of Israel forever" (Josh. 4:6–7).

Sometimes, actually a lot of times, you and I need stones of remembrance. We need tangible reminders of God's faithfulness in our life.

When we arrived at camp later that Friday evening, we threw our bags into the cabins and ran to the main building to begin the opening worship service. Once the service ended, we broke off into small groups that had been assigned for the weekend. I could not have handpicked a more diverse yet incredible group of girls.

The girls were from different life backgrounds, had different home situations, hung out in different friend groups, and each had a unique circumstance that had shaken her to the core. One girl recently lost her dad in an automobile accident. Another girl felt trapped by peer pressure and found herself making life-altering decisions. I could go on and on describing the real and painful things they were experiencing, but one specific girl stuck out to me. For anonymity, we will call her Liz.

Liz was a reserved girl. I was so excited that she was a part of our group, but she never talked. Each time we were together as a small group, she kept her head down, her long dark hair covering her face.

I understand that some people are uncomfortable in small group settings, so I did everything possible to make Liz feel at home. We might not hear from her during our group discussion, but I desperately wanted her to connect with the girls. I remember praying at the night's end that the Lord would open the doors for meaningful conversations with Liz.

We had morning sessions on Saturday and were dismissed for lunch and an afternoon of free time. This was the perfect opportunity to find Liz and hang out as a group. The only problem was I couldn't find her.

Dinner that evening was the first time I saw her since our afternoon of free time began. We connected as a small group after dinner, and once again Liz sat there, distancing herself from the conversation. I couldn't figure out what was running through her mind. Surely, she was listening and had something she wanted to say. Nope, nothing.

Sunday morning rolled around, and I felt like a mess. I was anxious, nervous, and badly wanted to back out of sharing. I skipped breakfast because my stomach was in knots. I paced back and forth in the building where the final worship service was scheduled, and I wrote in my journal: *"Jesus, give me the words to say. I have nothing to offer, but I'm asking you to do something this morning that can only be attributed back to you."*

Just a little advice: always be prepared for the Lord to answer such prayers.

As students piled into the room, the music began. I am confident we sang three songs, but the time passed so quickly it felt like we only sang half of one song.

The music faded, and I walked up to the stage with sweaty palms and my heart pounding.

The time was now.

I placed my Bible and note sheets on the table before me and spoke. Other than saying Jesus completely took over from that moment on, I can't explain what happened as I veered away from my notes and began sharing from God's Word what God placed on my heart.

As I finished, I will never forget the image as I scanned the worship center. Across the room, students had their heads bowed and were praying while others were literally on their faces before God. He was working in each person's life, including my own, but I had no way of knowing the extent of what he was doing in those moments.

We had about thirty minutes to break into small groups one last time before the weekend ended, and as we wrapped up our final group discussion, Liz was sitting off to the side. The Lord prompted me to ask her if there was any way I could be praying for her.

With her head lowered and her hair still covering her face, she said, "No, I need to deal with something on my own."

I had no idea what this meant, but one sentence led to the next, and she began to cry.

Liz was, unbeknown to me, one of the girls I had been praying for when we first left the church in Columbia, South Carolina, on Friday evening and were driving to camp for the weekend.

> *I know people are hurting on this trip just as much as I am right now. Students are facing situations that are just as difficult and painful as mine. Pour out your Spirit on all of us this weekend and change us! For those who don't know you as Savior, capture their hearts this weekend.*

I put my hand on Liz's shoulder and asked what was happening. Tears streamed down her face, and she began to open up for the first time all weekend. Liz was struggling. She was cutting herself and had attempted suicide twice. The following words out of her mouth will forever be engrained in my mind.

> *"Catherine, I'm scared my sister will end up in your shoes one day," she said. "I've watched you and learned from you all weekend. Seeing the hurt you are going through and the hope you have in Jesus makes me not want to do*

> *anything to end my life and hurt my family. There has to be a better way."*

As Liz spoke, I tried desperately to hold back my own tears but couldn't. We continued talking for another half hour while the students jumped on the buses and waited patiently to go home. Liz asked a few last questions, and with tears flowing like a river, she said, "I need Jesus. I want him to rescue me and be the Lord of my life."

At that very moment, Liz surrendered her life to Jesus and was saved.

This was the day things slowly started changing, not only for Liz as she began to find her identity in Christ but also for me as I began to see the truth of Genesis 50:20 coming to life.

God takes what the enemy intends for harm and uses it for good.

In Genesis, we read that Joseph was sold into slavery by his brothers, who were incredibly jealous of him. While Joseph was in slavery, the Lord was with him and gave him success in everything he did. He found favor in the eyes of the Egyptian officials and was put in charge of Potiphar's household. Potiphar was one of Pharaoh's officials. Think of him in today's world as being equivalent to an officer in the president's service.

During Joseph's time in Potiphar's house, he was falsely accused by Potiphar's wife of trying to have an affair with her, and as a result, he was thrown into prison. While in prison, the Lord was with Joseph, and he gained favor in the eyes of the prison warden. Joseph was then put in charge of everyone in the prison. Advance forward a bit in the story, and because Joseph could interpret a dream for Pharaoh, the king, he was released from prison and put in charge of the whole land of Egypt.

While Joseph oversaw the land of Egypt, the country enjoyed seven years of abundance, which he, having been warned in a dream that it would be seven years of abundance and then seven years of famine, wisely stored away copious amounts of food. When the seven years of famine came to pass, Joseph's brothers made their way to Egypt, knowing plenty of food could be found there. What they didn't know was that their brother, Joseph, whom they had sold into slavery years ago, was in charge of the land in Egypt. When Joseph saw his brothers for the first time, he pretended to be a stranger, knowing his brothers did not recognize him. Joseph would soon reveal himself to them, and they became indebted to Joseph. But Joseph spoke the profound words in Genesis 50:20 that still ring true today.

He said, "You intended to harm me, but God intended it for good to accomplish what is now being done, the saving of many lives."

The reality is that you and I have a real enemy who wants to destroy us, and if he cannot destroy us, he will try to discourage us and distract us. Satan intends to make us question God when we feel lost and cause us to run from God when we don't understand. But rest assured, God takes what is intended for evil and uses it for good. He takes our hurt and gives us hope. He takes our pain and provides us with peace. He takes the messes of our lives and uses them to accomplish his mission: the saving of many lives.

The enemy may win battles here on earth, but God wins the war for all of eternity.

I miss Barrett more than words can ever express, and I would do just about anything to have more time with him here on earth, but seeing what Jesus did in Liz's life gave me, for the first time since his death, a glimmer of hope. Jesus slowly began to bring me to a point where I can honestly say that if he uses Barrett's story to lead just one person to himself, it is all worth it. And that is precisely what he has done—again and again and again.

He takes our hurt, brings about healing, and then uses our story to share hope with others.

Whatever your story, Jesus can and will do the same for you. He takes our hurt, brings about healing, and then uses our story to share hope with others.

CHAPTER 11

Grief in the Desert

I returned to school after the fall retreat weekend, thanking Jesus for taking what the enemy intended for harm and using it for good. I knew God was doing exactly what he says he will do in his Word, as he began to use the most challenging season of my life for my good and his glory. However, it was only a matter of days before I found myself again in the woods, struggling to recognize his presence.

Grief is interesting, to say the least. I wish I could say otherwise, but there's no manual we can just pick up and read to make it more bearable. Every person experiences grief and processes it differently. It can be confusing and unpredictable. It has a way of producing a roller coaster of emotions. Honestly, it can make you feel mentally unhealthy at times. Everything seems okay and the next moment takes a dramatic turn, leaving us feeling as though we've sped downhill into a valley of turmoil. One minute, we may find ourselves praising Jesus; the next, we may find ourselves questioning everything about him.

This is where I found myself often in the months following my brother's death.

Running is one of my favorite things to do for both exercise and stress relief. I began running; well, let's be honest, I began jogging as a hobby in college and have continued doing so ever since. There was never a distinction in my mind between running and jogging until I went for a run with someone who ran track and cross-country in high school. As we started running, she told me to set the pace for the two of us. Once I settled into what I thought was a brisk run, I asked her what she thought about the pace. Big mistake. She looked at me and said, "Well, it's a little slow, but I'm good."

This was when I realized I was a jogger, not a runner.

My husband, Chris, and I got married in April 2011, and seven months into our marriage, I told him I wanted to train for a half marathon: 13.1 miles.

Together, we signed up for a race in December 2011 and immediately began searching online for a training program. We had no idea how long it takes to reasonably train for something like this, but we found a ten-week training program, and we were determined to be ready for the race by March 2012.

For ten straight weeks, we ran four times a week. Three of those days were short runs that ranged between four and seven miles, and every Saturday was a long run ranging from eight to twelve miles.

During this training period, I recognized a few things about myself that I had never thought of before.

First, I am goal driven. Many of us are. When I set my mind to accomplish something, I will do whatever it takes to meet that goal. Over ten weeks, I was determined not to miss one training day, and guess what . . . I didn't!

Second, I like to know where I am going. Most of us do. On the days when I had short runs, I mapped out the course so that I ran half the distance out before turning around and running the second half back home. This was simple. Long runs were different, though. I ran continuously in one direction, keeping my final destination in mind.

Three weeks before the race, I had to run ten miles for training, so I started at our house in West Columbia, South Carolina, and finished at our church in downtown Columbia before calling Chris to come and pick me up. It was undoubtedly a mental game, but knowing exactly where I was going and how far I had to go to get there gave me the drive and motivation to keep going until I finished.

Third, I like to know the purpose behind what I'm doing. Many of us do. Before training for the race, I had never run more than three miles during a workout. The only reason I would ever attempt to run eight, nine, or ten miles is to accomplish a specific goal. In this case, I ran long distances to finish a half marathon.

These three observations seem logical when it comes to everyday life. Having a goal in mind, knowing where you are going, and knowing the purpose behind your actions makes sense.

But what happens when the unexpected comes to pass? What happens when your plans are thrown out the window?

What happens when the path is uncertain and purpose seems lost?

This is exactly where I found myself after losing Barrett. Suddenly, I was in a long season of feeling like I was wandering through the wilderness with no clear direction. Sure, there were glimmers of hope along the way, like when Liz surrendered her life to Christ, but there were still more moments in those first six months where life felt dark and uncertain. The highs were definitely high, but the lows were incredibly low.

Webster's dictionary defines a *wilderness* as "a neglected, abandoned, or uninhabited place."

What imagery comes to mind when you think of a wilderness? Is it a wooded area filled with brush and trees? A park just over two miles from my house has been established in the middle of a forest. One could get lost for days if it weren't for a paved path amid the tree-filled area. The first time I walked this trail with a friend, I immediately thought about this wilderness type.

Perhaps you envision a desert. I encountered a desert for the first time while on a work trip in Arizona. It was exactly how I imagined it would be, but seeing it in person was captivating. Picture this: miles and miles of nothing but dry, red dirt. No water in sight and little plant life. I gazed at this in areas of Arizona as I drove around.

These images of the wilderness are often comparable to the state we find ourselves in when battling so many feelings that surface amid incredibly painful seasons of life—the feeling that you have to pretend you are okay, that you have to cope alone, that no one understands your struggle, that you're abandoned and defeated. All these feelings we experience tend to leave us dry and drained of life. They cloud our vision, so we cannot see the forest through the trees.

I found a journal entry written on December 5, 2008, exactly two months after Barrett met Jesus, that speaks to the depths of what I was feeling in my own wilderness:

> *Today is exactly two months since Barrett went home. I've felt up and down about everything but can't really express it. When people are around, I cover it up and make things appear as though they are okay. It's when I am alone that my mind races and I hurt so much.*
>
> *Nights are the hardest. It's at night when I think about things the most. I replay Barrett's phone call; I replay the conversations with the officers and paramedics; I replay the anger I felt toward his friends; and I replay the last goodbyes.*
>
> *As I sit here and write, tears are streaming, my heart is racing, and I am struggling to breathe. I feel empty and alone. It hurts, and no one knows. It's almost as though a ton of bricks is just sitting on my heart, and the weight won't disappear.*
>
> *I cannot get past the reality that my brother had a bad night and really took his life. When he didn't show up for Thanksgiving*

last month, it wasn't because he didn't want to or was off somewhere else. It was because he was no longer alive. He's really gone. He's not coming back.

. . . No one around me can understand how I feel. I'm overwhelmed and everything is not okay. Will I ever walk out of this dark forest? Will it ever be okay? I miss my brother and I don't know what to do; I don't know how to handle it. I'm empty, devastated, and unable to fully wrap my mind around the situation.

I must have cried myself to sleep that night while writing because the journal entry ends there.

The wilderness is an incredibly difficult place to be. It's discouraging, painful, and lonely, but thankfully we are never truly alone. My next journal entry speaks to the presence and faithfulness of God amid my journey through the wilderness of Barrett's death:

December 6, 2008

Father,

I just woke up and opened my Bible. Jeremiah 31 appeared before me, and you are using these two verses to speak to my heart:

"I will turn their mourning into gladness; I will give them comfort and joy instead of sorrow." (v. 13)

"I have loved you with an everlasting love;
I have drawn you with unfailing kindness."
(v. 3)

Looking back at my journal entries written less than eight hours apart, it would seem that I had lost my mind. One evening I was hopeless; the following day I was hopeful. In a matter of hours, it seemed like God was both distant and present.

How is this possible? Is this normal? Or is something wrong with me?, I wondered.

Our ever-changing emotions at the drop of a dime can make us question our sanity. I did the same until I realized I wasn't the only one. One night, I was flipping through the book of Psalms in the Bible, and I noticed something peculiar about David. His heart wavered as much as mine did. In Psalm 9, David writes, "I will give thanks to you, LORD, with all my heart; I will tell of all your wonderful deeds. I will be glad and rejoice in you; I will sing praises of your name, O Most High" (vv. 1–2). Meanwhile, Psalm 10 begins with these words, also presumably penned by David, "Why, LORD, do you stand far off? Why do you hide yourself in times of trouble?"

Look at Psalm 12:7, where David writes, "You, LORD, will keep the needy safe and will protect us forever from the wicked." Just two verses later, in Psalm 13:1–2 we read, "How long, LORD? Will you forget me forever? How long will you hide your face from me? How long must I wrestle with my thoughts and day after day have sorrow in my heart?"

While the chapters of Psalms are not structured chronologically, we can still gather that David's life was met with highs and lows. Within those mountaintop and valley experiences, his temperament toward God fluctuated. At times, David easily worshipped God and marveled at his faithfulness. Other times, he, like us, questioned the presence of God. Job, Abraham, Habakkuk, and many others that we read about in the Bible found themselves doing the same thing.

The good news is that although our emotions waver in the grief cycle, God does not. He is unchanging, always near, and forever faithful. Hebrews 13:8 says Jesus Christ is the same yesterday, today, and forever. He is with us in the good moments and with us in the worst of moments. He sees, cares for, and meets us where we are. And as seen in my journal entry on December 6, he never ceases to speak the right words to our hearts at just the right moments.

Psalm 119:105 says, "Your word is a lamp to my feet, a light on my path."

It's been a long time since I've walked on a trail of any kind in the dark, but every night before I go to sleep, I grab my phone and turn on the flashlight before opening the door to each of my kids' bedrooms. I enter their room and point the light down toward the floor so that I do not trip as I make my way over to their beds to tuck them in one last time, kiss them on the cheek, and tell them good night as they are sound asleep. I then turn back toward the door, shining the light on the floor until I exit their rooms. The flashlight on my phone is the lamp to my feet and the light to my path while I quietly try to maneuver around toys, books, and clothes that should have been put away, as I slip in and out of their bedrooms.

Similarly, the Bible is a lamp to our feet and a light to our path as we navigate the unexpected tragedies and trials we encounter in this adventure called life. God has a special way of using his Word to shine light in our darkness and provide hope amid our suffering.

> We may not always know where we are going or the purpose behind our circumstances, but we can know that God is present. He is with us, and he is at work amid our wilderness.

No matter what you may be feeling right now, hang in there, friend! We may not always know where we are going or the purpose behind our circumstances, but we can know that God is present. He is with us, and he is at work amid our wilderness. He can take what the enemy intends for harm in your life and use it for good. And while you may struggle to see what the purpose could be right now, you can find encouragement and light as you open the Bible and allow Jesus to speak directly to your heart.

Chapter 12

Truth to Behold

The first twelve months are the hardest; this is no surprise to anyone who has walked through *loss*. After the initial shock of Barrett's death, my family relived the pain repeatedly as we experienced the "firsts" of the year ahead. The first Thanksgiving he wasn't sitting around the table with us, the first Christmas he wasn't opening gifts with us, the first Mother's Day he wasn't there to hug my mom and tell her he loved her, the first birthday we didn't get to celebrate him turning another year older, the first time I tried to call and check in with him out of habit before remembering he wasn't going to pick up the phone. All of these occasions, although rarely discussed, heightened our awareness of a huge void left in the depths of our hearts.

It makes sense that the "firsts" of every occasion and anniversary, however big or small, are the hardest after losing someone, but most people don't acknowledge the long-term struggle ahead. I can't remember a single time anyone tried to prepare me for what would be a full year and more of unrelenting grief.

Instead, I was told:

> *"The first few days are the hardest because everything seems surreal."*
>
> *"Catherine, just give yourself time. In a few weeks, it will get easier."*
>
> *"Once you return to your normal routine, things will be better."*

I wish someone would have felt the liberty to say, *"Catherine, these are painful days, and it may be like this for a long time. That's okay. Allow yourself the time to grieve."*

The void left by Barrett's death was difficult to endure. Trying to figure out how to cope with that void was just as hard and sometimes resulted in more significant turmoil.

We all respond differently while suffering. While I internalized everything and tried to cope quietly with Barrett's suicide, my sister will tell you that she dealt with Barrett's death differently. Kimberly loves Jesus and, to this day, lives for him, but losing Barrett took a toll on her, and she ran from Jesus for nearly two years. The enemy does everything he can to kick us while we are down, which is exactly what he did to her and the rest of my family.

First Peter 5:8–9 warns us, "Be alert and of sober mind. Your enemy the devil prowls around like a roaring lion looking for someone to devour. Resist him, standing firm in the faith, because you know that the family of believers throughout the world is undergoing the same kind of sufferings."

Peter, knowing we are more vulnerable to Satan's attacks when we are suffering, warns us to be alert. Satan is just waiting for us to become so distracted by our circumstances that we take our eyes off Jesus so he can slip in and devour us. Peter further instructs us to stand firm in the faith. To stand firm is to stay focused on Jesus. We must constantly remind ourselves of who Jesus is while allowing him to help us and teach us along the way.

Whether we've known Jesus for most of our life, known him for a short while, or maybe you're reading this and you don't know him as Savior yet, these three truths are worth learning and clinging to over and over again.

Jesus Is Not Far Away

Psalm 34:18 says, "The LORD is close to the brokenhearted and saves those who are crushed in spirit." Contrary to how we sometimes feel, Jesus is not some distant, far-off, unapproachable God who does not comprehend where we are or what we're going through. But instead, he sees us and meets us where we are. He is in the trenches of hurt with us.

Contrary to how we sometimes feel, Jesus is not some distant, far-off, unapproachable God who does not comprehend where we are or what we're going through.

One of Jesus's promises is that he will never leave or forsake us. This means that even in our most painful moments, he is near. And not only is he near, but he is speaking on our behalf to God the Father when we can't muster up the words to say on our own.

After losing Barrett, there were nights when I simply prayed, "*Jesus, I don't even know what to say right now, but I need your help.*" To be honest, there are still nights that I find myself praying this same prayer. Romans 8:26 says, "The Spirit helps us in our weakness. We do not know what we ought to pray for, but the Spirit himself intercedes for us with wordless groans." Whether we are experiencing more emotions than we can articulate or simply have no words at all, Jesus meets us where we are. Friend, you are not alone; he is close to the brokenhearted.

Total dependence on Jesus is indispensable.

Psalm 121:1–2 says, "I lift up my eyes to the mountains—where does my help come from? My help comes from the LORD, the Maker of heaven and earth."

Even though there were more extended and lonely nights of confusion than I would like to admit, God used these moments not only to remind me of my need to depend on him, but also to help me see that I can depend on him. There was not one time when I reached out to Jesus that he failed to respond. Looking back, seeing how he provided exactly what I needed at just the right times is refreshing. Sometimes it was through his Word. Sometimes it was through encouragement from friends, and other times through simple waves of peace that passed all understanding. He is our help at all times and in all things.

I recently spoke to a friend who unexpectedly lost her son, and she said, "Catherine, my heart hurts, and some days I can barely put one foot in front of the other. I don't know how people go through these things without Jesus. I couldn't do it." I could not agree with her more. "God is," as mentioned in Psalm 46:1, "our refuge and strength, an ever-present help in trouble."

A contemporary Christian song sung by Matt Maher called "Lord, I Need You"[6] unashamedly confesses our constant need for Jesus. Whether we realize it or not, every hour of every day, we need him. While we often get caught in the trap of trying to muscle our way through life on our own, he doesn't expect us to, nor does he want us to. Jesus is the only one who can give rest to the weary, comfort to the hurting, and hope to the hopeless. We desperately need him.

Trust placed in Jesus will never be misplaced trust.

Isaiah 26:4 says, "Trust in the LORD forever, for the LORD, the LORD himself, is the Rock eternal."

At no point in my life has Jesus ever broken my trust, yet I find him having to teach me to fully trust him repeatedly.

In the Bible we read that the Israelites were caught in the cycle of having a need in the wilderness, questioning God, seeing God provide for that need, praising and thanking him, having another need arise, and yet forgetting how he provided in the past while questioning his faithfulness all over again.

This is me. Maybe it is also you. We've seen God do things in our lives that can only be attributed to him. We've watched him open doors that only he can open and provide in ways that only he can provide, and yet we still have a hard time trusting him the next time uncertainty arises.

Over that first year without Barrett, Proverbs 3:5–6 became my life verse and still is to this day. It says, "Trust in the LORD with all your heart and lean not on your own understanding; in all your ways submit to him, and he will make your paths straight."

To trust someone is to have complete confidence in that person. To trust the Lord with all our heart is to have that same confidence in Jesus, knowing he has everything under control and our best interest in mind. It is fully believing he will take care of us. We're instructed in Proverbs 3 not to rely on our own understanding because we can't see the whole picture like God does. Instead, we are to seek him in all our ways, and in doing so, we allow him to take the lead in our lives and fulfill his purpose in our lives.

Whether you are one month in or twelve months in, walking through a wilderness of any kind is never easy; it requires faith. Faith is simply trusting Jesus, even when things don't make sense. Hebrews 11:1 says, "Now faith is confidence in what we hope for and assurance about what we do not see." In these moments, we learn the most and grow the deepest.

How can you trace God's hand at work in your circumstances? What are you learning along the way?

CHAPTER 13

Pure Joy

James 1:2 says, "Consider it pure joy, my brothers and sisters, whenever you face trials of many kinds." That's a joke, right? Is it even possible to consider it not just joy but pure joy when we face the most difficult trials of our lives?

There are several occasions where I recall experiencing pure joy. April 30, 2011, was one of those times. I married the love of my life, my best friend, and my partner in ministry—Chris Renfro. On December 17, 2015, Chris and I had our first baby, Isaac, and despite thirty-six hours of labor and an emergency C-section, pure joy seems like an understatement. Nearly twenty months later, on August 13, 2017, our little girl, Ava, was born three weeks early. It was, again, a day like none other. I was supposed to be at church that morning, and Chris was just moments away from teaching middle and high school students when I called him and said we needed to get to the hospital quickly. He rushed home, friends of ours took care of Isaac, and off to the hospital we went. When we arrived at the hospital in Atlanta, Georgia, Chris dropped me off at the door and left to park the car.

One of the greatest moments happened while I waited for him to enter. The lady at the check-in desk and I began talking about church and Jesus. As we waited for my name to be called, I shared the message Chris was supposed to teach our students that morning, and she lit up with joy. She shared a personal story and said Chris's message that morning was intended for her. That is just one of many examples of how Jesus works in the details of our circumstances. Just as we were wrapping up the conversation, a nurse called me back to a room, and within an hour Ava was born. Fast-forward seven years and we adopted our third child, Elijah. Pure joy.

These moments pop into my mind as I think about *joy*, not seasons of trials, tragedy, and suffering. However, joy is often misrepresented as being associated with happy moments and fun occasions. Realistically, joy and happiness should be treated totally different.

Happiness is temporal, ever shifting, and utterly dependent on our circumstances, whereas joy is a gift rooted in God the Father. Joy is not an emotion that changes with the tide but an attitude of the heart anchored in Jesus.

So, is it possible to consider it pure joy when we face trials of many kinds? When we lose someone to suicide? When cancer strikes? When a job is lost? When a friend betrays us?

The answer is yes. Yes, we can consider it pure joy when we face trials of many kinds, but we must continue reading the first chapter of James to put this command into perspective.

James says, "Consider it pure joy, my brothers and sisters, whenever you face trials of many kinds, because you know that the testing of your faith produces perseverance.

Let perseverance finish its work so that you may be mature and complete, not lacking anything" (James 1:2–4).

In other words, there's a purpose behind our pain.

The question is: What is the purpose?

Trials test our faith. In Deuteronomy 8, God allows the Israelites to journey through a wilderness for forty years. Why? The Bible says to humble them. To test them. To see what was in their hearts and whether they would keep his commands.

Trials reveal our faith. My brother's suicide tested my faith. It shook me to the core and later caused me to evaluate whether there was a distinction between my stated beliefs and my actual beliefs. You see, stated beliefs are what we say we believe, whereas actual beliefs are revealed by our practices. Theologian Henry Thiessen says, "Men act according to what they really believe, not according to what they merely pretend to believe."[7]

In the trenches our faith is tested, and our actual beliefs are on display. Leading up to October 5, 2008, I would, without hesitation, say that God is sovereign. I would agree that he is good, faithful, and trustworthy. He is all the things! But losing my brother tested my faith in a way that caused me to question everything I knew to be true of God.

Thankfully, a season of questioning God doesn't mean we automatically fail the test of faith. God can withstand our questions; even more so, he welcomes our questions as they can lead us to seek him.

Trials test our faith, but the *testing* of our *faith*, as James says, produces perseverance. Perseverance is the ability to keep going despite the obstacles that arise. Think about Job, a man in the Bible who lost everything. Job was a wealthy farmer who had a family and loved God. Job 1:1 says, "This man was blameless and upright; he feared God and shunned evil." Things were going well for Job, and suddenly everything changed when he unexpectedly lost his wealth, family, and health. Everything dear to Job was now gone. Talk about a test of faith. Job had no idea why God allowed this to happen. He was sad, hurt, confused, and had lots of questions. Three of his friends said this must have occurred due to sin in his life. Elihu said Job must have become proud and that this was God's way of punishing and humbling him.

> A season of questioning God doesn't mean we automatically fail the test of faith.

Job agonized over his situation but never gave up on God, even amid his suffering. Job models the kind of trust we are to have. He perseveres in the depths of despair and focuses on the prize: God himself. We, too, can do the same. Because hope doesn't lie in our family, friends, circumstances, or experiences but solely in Jesus, we can persevere amid the wilderness while encountering the joy Jesus alone offers.

Don't give up. What you've been through, what you're going through, or what you will go through is not the end of your story. Instead, we learn the most and grow the deepest in these chapters of life. In these chapters of our story, we are challenged and tested; all the while, God is working to make us mature and complete.

What does "mature and complete" mean? It means God is working amid our circumstances to sanctify us, to make us more like Jesus while also preparing us to be used by Jesus for his glory.

I once heard, "God prepares you for what he has prepared for you." This thought is revolutionary. Just think about it; God is working behind the scenes in every facet of your life to teach you, stretch you, change you, and equip you for what he has in store for you.

No one loves the wilderness. No one loves the experiences of hopelessness, confusion, pain, and uncertainty that come along with the wilderness. But in these moments where our faith is tested, we have an opportunity to see God on display.

Until my brother's death, I can only think of one other time in my life when my faith was really tested. I was a sophomore in high school, and a close friend of mine lost his battle with cancer. February 6, 2002, was a tough day for all of us at school, but we knew Brandon had a relationship with Jesus, which changed everything. What was already a painful week became even more difficult just two days later when another friend was killed in a car accident.

Talk about testing. Is this real life? How does this happen? These two situations led to many questions and doubts but also to lots of conversations about Jesus. Looking back, I can trace the hand of God as he orchestrated divine moments along the way.

Brandon's love for Jesus was exuded through his life. Even while he was in and out of the hospital during his cancer journey, he never stopped loving Jesus and pointing others to him. As a result of his life and love for the Lord, my other friend put his faith in Jesus the same day of Brandon's death, not knowing that just two days later he would be driving to school, hit a patch of black ice on the road, lose control of his car, and have his life suddenly come to an end.

February 6 and February 8, 2002 were incredibly dark days, but despite the hurt in so many of us, we had a choice to make. It is a choice you and I must make regularly as life takes us by surprise. Will we lean into Jesus during these tests of faith, or will we run from him? I won't pretend to be extra spiritual with you and say I have never chosen the latter. But I will tell you that leaning into Jesus, even in the most painful circumstances, is life giving. As the author and perfecter of our faith, Jesus provides all we need to navigate the wilderness so that we are not only sustained until the end but also learn and grow to become more like Jesus in the process.

This was a lesson I learned in 2002 and one that I would relearn in the months and years following Barrett's death in 2008.

While we may not be happy amid hurt, we can be joyful knowing that he who began a good work in us will continue it until the day of Christ Jesus (Phil. 1:6).

Friend, let me remind you that even though you cannot always see it, there is purpose in your pain.

Consider it pure joy knowing that Jesus is not finished with you yet!

Chapter 14

A Story Worth Sharing

God has a way of using our most difficult seasons to produce our most fruitful seasons. It's one thing to believe this; it's another to experience and understand it.

In February 2014, my husband, Chris, planned a Valentine's getaway weekend in Atlanta, Georgia. Chris grew up in a large city, and I grew up in a small town. Every now and then, we would talk about different places we could see ourselves living and places we definitely did not want to live. I don't think we ever agreed on a location until this particular getaway weekend.

> *"Hey, Chris!" I said.*
>
> *"What?" he answered.*
>
> *"I don't know why, but I think I could see us living in Atlanta one day."* Believe it or not, Chris agreed!
>
> *"Yea? I think living in Atlanta would be fun!" he said.*

We enjoyed the rest of our weekend together in the city, drove home, and didn't think anything about it. After all, we loved where we lived and had no intentions of moving anywhere.

About six months later, God began working in ways we could have never imagined. Chris received a phone call about a job opportunity at a church in Alpharetta, Georgia, a northern suburb of Atlanta. We both said it would be cool to live in Atlanta, but I didn't want to move there, right? That would mean moving out of my comfort zone and starting over. Who wants to do that?! We had the most incredible friends and a solid church family, and honestly, we were coming off our best summer yet in student ministry.

I anticipated Chris declining the job offer on multiple occasions, but each time I did, Jesus would do something in return, making clear he wanted us to move. So we did. Within about three months, we were living on the outskirts of the city we agreed we could see ourselves living in one day.

Having grown up in Kansas City, Chris was used to city life. On the other hand, I had never lived in a vast city, but for some reason I was drawn to it. I love everything about it except for the traffic. Let's be honest: Atlanta traffic is a gift from the enemy.

Our first few years in Atlanta were unlike anything we had ever experienced. The pace of life was different, the opportunities were different, the culture was different, and the ministry was different. But even in a crowd of differences, one thing was the same—the brokenness surrounding us.

The community we were now a part of had just experienced four teen suicides, and sadly, several more occurred over the next couple of years. I could have never imagined, when Chris and I said yes to moving here, how quickly God would begin using the story he had been writing in my life to speak into the lives of friends who became family and students in our new ministry. These tragedies broke my heart to the core as memories of my own brother flooded my mind. The empathy I felt for these families was heavy.

On several occasions, I sat across the table and listened as friends and relatives of the deceased asked the same questions I asked when Barrett took his life.

> *"Why do these things happen?"*
>
> *"Why doesn't God stop them from happening?"*
>
> *"Why my family?"*
>
> *"Will the hurt ever go away?"*
>
> *"Where was God?"*

I nodded in agreement as they tried their best to express the pain that was too hard to articulate into words. And I welled up with tears, knowing there wasn't a thing I could say that would make the situation any better or easier. I still searched for answers myself, and I still felt the pain that never really subsided. I guess time was the only thing that set me apart in these conversations. Whereas their losses were recent, it had been six years since Barrett's death, which meant six years further down the road of processing and learning to look to Jesus for light amid darkness and hope while suffering.

I didn't have answers to give, but I had the experience to share, and I am forever grateful for how Jesus took my story of brokenness and used it to help others know the hope that is found in Jesus alone.

I will never forget the Thursday night I was invited to speak at a student-led faith gathering. I was sitting in the back row, and a high school girl walked in just as the band began leading worship.

"*Hey!*" I said.

She said hi back.

Assuming she had been to the gathering before, I whispered, "*They just got started. Feel free to go sit with your friends if you want.*"

She didn't know a single person in the room, so I invited her to sit with me. She didn't know I was the speaker for the evening, and I didn't know anything about her, but we stood in the back and worshipped Jesus together.

The last song ended, and the emcee for the evening called me to the stage. Standing up and walking to the front, I quietly prayed, "*Jesus, do a work that only you can do tonight. Amen.*"

I spoke for about twenty-five minutes, and as I began wrapping up the message, the Holy Spirit prompted me to give these students a chance to respond to the gospel. So I did. Two students surrendered their lives to Jesus, one being the girl who came in late and sat down beside me in the back row. We talked for a few minutes afterward, and she shared with me the darkness she was wading through and the similarities of our stories. She said she wasn't sure why she felt like she needed to be there that evening, but she overheard some other students talking about the gathering at school earlier in the day and decided to check it out. She entered the room that night broken and searching for hope, and she left knowing Jesus and experiencing life.

The truth is, we are all broken people. When God created the world, he created everything in perfection. Go back to Genesis 1 in the Bible and read for yourself. God's design was flawless. He created everything from the heavens and the earth to the plants, animals, and humans that inhabit it. "God saw all he had made, and it was very good" (Gen. 1:31).

When God created us, man and woman, he created us, as Genesis 1:27 says, in his own image. You and I were created specifically for a purpose: to know God and enjoy him as we live with him and for him. God's original design was that we would live with him and honor him with our relationships, finances, jobs, and every other aspect of our lives. But something happened. God placed the first man, Adam, and his wife, Eve, in the garden of Eden to work and care for the land. They had free rein of the entire garden with one exception. God told the two, "You are free to eat from any tree in the garden; but you must not eat from the tree of the knowledge of good and evil, for when you eat from it you will certainly die" (Gen. 2:16–17).

The truth is, we are all broken people.

If you continue reading in Genesis 3, you see that Adam and Eve did the one thing they were asked not to do; they chose to eat from the tree of the knowledge of good and evil, and from then on, everything changed for us. Sin, which is disobedience to God, entered the world and altered God's design for you and for me. The relationship he intended for us to have with him was broken, and our world was turned upside down. His design for every aspect of life was affected.

Sin has led all of us to spiritual brokenness.

Sometimes our brokenness is a direct result of our innate desire to do things our way rather than God's. Other times our brokenness is caused by the ripple effect of someone else's decisions. And sometimes, there is no explanation other than that we live in an imperfect world. In all three scenarios, we find ourselves hurting and desperately needing hope, searching for relief, and searching for answers. You may be walking through a season where you need help. You need hope.

The good news is that there is hope, and his name is Jesus. First Peter 1:3–5 says: "Praise be to the God and Father of our Lord Jesus Christ! In his great mercy he has given us new birth into a living hope through the resurrection of Jesus Christ from the dead, and into an inheritance that can never perish, spoil or fade. This inheritance is kept in heaven for you, who through faith are shielded by God's power until the coming of the salvation that is ready to be revealed in the last time."

When sin entered the world, God could have easily dropped his pen and closed the book, leaving us with an inevitably hopeless ending. But he didn't. Out of a love so deep and compassion so wide, he made a way for your story and my story to be written with the certainty of a beautiful ending. John 3:16, the most well-known verse in the Bible, explains that "God so loved the world that he gave his one and only Son, that whoever believes in him shall not perish but have eternal life."

Every life has a story, but not every story has life.

You see, the narrative of our story changes when we realize the life-giving news of John 3:16 and place our faith in Jesus. This is where our story begins, the moment we put our pen down and allow God to begin writing our story. In these moments, God takes our brokenness and begins redeeming our story through faith in Jesus. In that moment we are given life in exchange for death, forgiveness in exchange for punishment, and living hope in exchange for despair.

Though painful, my story has life because of what Jesus has done for me. My brother's story, though cut short, has life because of what Jesus did for him. This young lady who walked through the doors of a student gathering that Thursday evening now has a story of life because of her faith in what Jesus did for her.

You never know who Jesus is going to have cross your path, but you can be sure that every person needs to be pointed to Jesus. The story Jesus is writing in your life may be what he uses to do just that. Though the chapters may be long and difficult, it is worth it.

Before 2008, I only knew of one family who had been affected by the loss of a loved one to suicide. I never heard conversations about the topic, and I certainly didn't know of anyone who struggled with suicidal thoughts. However, my brother's death on Sunday, October 5, was the start of what seemed like a domino effect. Suddenly, similar situations were popping up all around me. Within six months of losing Barrett, I encountered three different situations where suicide was talked about, attempted, and in one case, carried out. Then, when we moved to Georgia, it began to feel like an epidemic.

I had no idea this was such a prevalent struggle among many people, but my eyes quickly opened. Research shows that suicide is one of the leading causes of death in the United States.[8] Every occurrence seemed to pour salt in the open wounds I have from losing Barrett, but at the same time, I felt the need to do something, anything, to help. The desire was there, but the problem was that I didn't know how to help. All I had was an aching heart, the experience of feeling left behind, and my ever-developing story of learning to trust God amid this wilderness. What I didn't realize at the time was that this *was* more than enough.

Second Corinthians 1:3–5 says, "Praise be to the God and Father of our Lord Jesus Christ, the Father of compassion and the God of all comfort, who comforts us in all our troubles, so that we can comfort those in any trouble with the comfort we ourselves receive from God. For just as we share abundantly in the sufferings of Christ, so also our comfort abounds through Christ."

You may remember me mentioning earlier that my friend and college mentor, Taryn, wrote Scripture on a stack of Post-it notes and gave them to me soon after Barrett's death. It was a season where I was on the receiving end of this truth found in 2 Corinthians 1 as God took the story he had been writing in Taryn's life and used it to comfort me as he was writing a challenging chapter in my personal story.

God had comforted Taryn; she comforted me, and I had no idea how the tides would turn; one day, God would use my story to comfort others walking on similar paths.

Your circumstances may be painful, but they are not purposeless. If you have a relationship with Jesus, God is writing your story and intends for it to be shared. You may not see it now, but you may be surprised at just how many people around you have either walked in your shoes or are currently walking in your shoes and are searching for hope amid their wilderness.

Soon after moving to Georgia in 2014, I was at an event where several people shared cardboard testimonies. They had written one word on each side of a piece of cardboard that illustrated Jesus's transforming work in their life. These testimonies spoke of redemption from abusive relationships, reconciliation for broken families, freedom from addictions, and several other stories. At the end of the night, several of those people were approached by others who were walking through similar situations and were encouraged as a result of seeing what Jesus had the power to do. This is what the body of Christ does; we comfort one another with the comfort we have received from God. Comfort is a gift from the Father that keeps on giving.

Your circumstances may be painful, but they are not purposeless.

I told you in the preface of this book that it's taken me a long time to muster the courage to sit down and write this story. I started writing. I quit writing. I started writing again. I quit again. This happened dozens of times, but there are two specific instances where I opened my computer, began typing, and soon after received a phone call. One phone call was from a friend who had just lost a family member to suicide. The other was from someone contemplating suicide. The timing of writing and receiving these calls was rattling to me but not surprising to God. He was now allowing me to be on the giving end of 2 Corinthians 1:4, "who comforts us, . . . so that we can comfort others with the comfort we ourselves receive."

After both conversations, I found the verses of Scripture that Taryn wrote for me on Post-it notes when I was in college and emailed those same verses of Scripture to these two friends.

Just as Taryn reached out to me after Barrett's passing, there may be someone you, too, can reach out to one day. The details of your story are personal, but the message of hope found only in Jesus is universal. The gospel is for everyone, and your impact on those who hear it from you may be eternal.

CHAPTER 15

A Willing Spirit

If there is one tactic the enemy uses repeatedly in an attempt to paralyze us, it's fear. Fear of uncertainty. Fear of judgment. Fear of ____________ (you fill in the blank). For me, it's a fear of failure.

It's no coincidence that whenever God leads us to do something bigger than ourselves, we begin to think of every reason it can't be done. We see the same thing happening throughout Scripture. God called Moses to lead the Israelites out of Egypt, but Moses claimed his speech impediment hindered him. Jonah was called to preach against the wickedness in Nineveh, but he ran the other way. God told Gideon he would lead the Israelites to victory through him, but Gideon tested God twice before he would believe God. Abraham and Sarah struggled to believe God would give them a son because of their old age. The list of examples could go on and on, but in each scenario, God did exactly what he said he would do.

Satan has a way of planting seeds of doubt, knowing that doubt decreases faith and increases fear. Amid doubt, our inadequacy is maximized, and Jesus's sufficiency is minimized. The story becomes about what we cannot do rather than what Jesus can do.

During my junior year of college, the Lord gave me the greatest group of friends who met every Sunday night to hang out and have dinner together. This group slightly changed over time due to people graduating and relocating, but the tradition continued for years. This gathering of believers was a place of celebrating successes, carrying burdens, and growing spiritually. Some of my greatest moments of encouragement came from this group, as well as my biggest challenges to step out of my comfort zone and live by faith in Jesus.

I will never forget a conversation that happened one night around the dinner table as we talked through Barrett's death. They asked me questions about how I was coping and ways I was seeing or struggling to see Jesus at work. These conversations played a vital role in my journey through the wilderness because these friends could see the bigger picture and speak truth into my life when I couldn't see past the moment. At the close of one of our discussions, my friend, Michael, left me with a verse from the Bible to chew on that radically impacted my faith. Habakkuk 1:5 says, "Look at the nations and watch—and be utterly amazed. For I am going to do something in your days that you would not believe, even if you were told."

To avoid taking this verse out of context, looking at what was happening at the time that would elicit such a response is essential. Habakkuk, who lived in Judah, was watching violence and corruption prevail all around him, and he couldn't understand why God was allowing it to happen. Out of a broken heart, Habakkuk asked God, "How long . . . must I call for help, but you do not listen?" (v. 2) and "Why do you tolerate wrongdoing?" (v. 3). Habakkuk was angry and hurt. The Lord then responded, letting Habakkuk know that he would do things that would amaze him. One of these things God referred to was that he would raise up the Babylonians to punish Judah for their wicked ways. This made absolutely no sense to Habakkuk, knowing the Babylonians were even worse than his people in Judah, who had turned away from God. Habakkuk continued asking questions about how it would all play out, and God responded with answers.

What is even more amazing than God's answers to Habakkuk's questions is that the people saw God's words come to fruition in their lifetime. The Lord did, in fact, raise up the Babylonians to power, and he used them to help the people of Judah return to himself. Later, the Babylonians fell from power, just as God said they would.

The promise and the message found in Habakkuk fuel our faith. The message is that God is in complete control and at work, fulfilling his purposes, even when we do not understand the *how* and the *why*. And the promise is that he will do things we wouldn't believe even if we were told.

We, like Habakkuk, have similar questions that are specific to our own circumstances. Whether it's a failing marriage, a battle with illness, a rebellious child, the loss of a job, the death of a loved one, or whatever the case may be, our questions tend to be, "God, why are you letting this happen? How long must I call for help, but you do not answer?"

I think about this story, and I'm reminded of a song called "Through the Fire." The idea of this song is that God never promised life would be void of trials and hardships, but he did promise to show up and walk with us through them.

We can walk confidently and with courage, knowing Jesus is at work on our behalf to accomplish his will in his way.

As Michael talked about Habakkuk 1:5 that evening, he told me to mark his words—Jesus would do something I wouldn't believe in my life even if I were told. As I write this book over a decade later, I am in awe of all that Jesus has done despite my lack of understanding and, at times, disbelief.

As Habakkuk brought his concerns to God, he also brought a willing spirit to listen and learn as God worked in and through his life. This is a game changer for each of us.

A willing spirit opens the doors of our hearts to seek Jesus and be a part of his work as he uses the story he's writing in our lives for his glory.

In the fall of 2021, I was at an event where the artists who produced and sang the song "Rescue" were leading worship. *This is the song that was on the radio the night my dad and I rushed to Barrett's house after he shot himself.* The set list that evening even included that song!

After the event, I went over to talk with the band and shared the story of hearing their song in the early morning of October 5, 2008, and its impact on me in those last moments of my brother's life. I also asked for permission to use the story in this book. One of the guys said, "You should absolutely use it" and began to tear up. He then proceeded to share about a suicide loss someone near him experienced two weeks before our conversation and asked, "Would you mind praying for us? You can do so in a way that not many know how."

What a God moment!

All I can say is that only Jesus can orchestrate these types of encounters, but he does. Jesus knows our stories and crosses our paths with people who need to hear our stories and be pointed to him.

Jesus tends to do things we could never fathom alone in our lives. These are the best moments because they are beyond our control and complete God stories. Ephesians 3:20–21 says, "Now to him who is able to do immeasurably more than all we ask or imagine, according to his power that is work within us, to him be glory in the church and in Christ Jesus throughout all generations, for ever and ever!"

The key word in this verse is "him." Jesus will do more than we can ever ask or imagine. All we have to do is be willing. Willing to listen, learn, and follow. Second Timothy 1:7 says, "For the Spirit God gave us does not make us timid, but gives us power, love and self-discipline."

In the Bible, Moses, Jonah, Gideon, Sarah, Abraham, Paul, and many others have one thing in common. Once they put their yes on the table and were willing to obey God, they all succeeded in doing things that were completely bigger than themselves. Moses led the Israelites out of Egypt, Gideon led them to victory, Sarah and Abraham had their first son, Isaac, and Paul preached the gospel and watched thousands be saved.

The enemy will use fear, doubt, pain, and more to hold you back from what God has in store for you. Don't let this be the case. Instead, let's be willing and be ready!

> Jesus knows our stories and crosses our paths with people who need to hear our stories and be pointed to him.

This journey our family has been on since Barrett took his life has been beyond painful, but out of it has come a lesson that is worth sharing: God is near to us, he is faithful to us, and he provides for us.

In Matthew 14, the disciples are in a boat on the lake, and Jesus approaches them while walking on water. The disciples were terrified, but Jesus said to them, "Take courage! It is I. Don't be afraid" (v. 27). His disciple, Peter, replied, "Lord if it is you, . . . tell me to come to you on the water" (v. 28). Jesus commanded Peter to get out of the boat, and so he did. Scripture says, "Then Peter got down out of the boat, walked on the water and came toward Jesus" (v. 29).

Anytime Jesus speaks to us, he calls for a response. He wants us to trust him. He wants us to follow him. He wants us to be obedient to him.

What is he calling you to do next? Is he calling you to trust him? Is he calling you to follow him? Is he calling you to share your journey with others to point them to him? A neighbor of mine has been telling me for a while now to step out of the boat and allow Jesus to use this book in ways that only he can. You may need to be encouraged just as I did. Will you step out of the boat, trust Jesus, and let him work in and through your life as only he can?

Conclusion

A Note to the Reader

I don't know you. I don't know your story. But I know who does. His name is Jesus. My prayer for you after reading this book is that you see his love for you and the hope he offers to you. Circumstances may or may not turn out as we would like, but Jesus's goodness and faithfulness are not dependent on our circumstances. He sees you. He loves you. He cares for you, and he wants a relationship with you. I pray you take one step closer to him after reading this book and seeing how he really does work all things for the good of those who love him and are called according to his purpose (Rom. 8:28).

I would love to hear from you if I can be praying for you. Email me at Catherine1513@gmail.com, and I will be more than honored to pray for you. I am praying for you even now as I write this.

About the Author

Catherine Renfro is a pastor's wife, a mom, and serves as the National Director of Women's Evangelism at the North American Mission Board. She and her husband, Chris Renfro, were married in April of 2011 and have three awesome kiddos. Catherine graduated from The University of South Carolina in 2008 with a Bachelor of Arts in Journalism and Mass Communications and from Southeastern Baptist Theological Seminary in 2010 with a Master of Arts in Christian Education and Biblical Counseling after being called to vocational ministry at the age of twenty-two. She has been serving in full time ministry ever since. She has a passion for seeing lost people come to know Jesus and for saved people to live out their purpose of making Jesus known.

Notes

1. "Suicide," World Health Organization, August 29, 2024, https://www.who.int/news-room/fact-sheets/detail/suicide.

2. "Suicide," National Institute of Mental Health, accessed December 15, 2024, https://www.nimh.nih.gov/health/statistics/suicide.

3. "Held" written by Christa Nicole Wells and recorded by Natalie Grant.

4. "You Wouldn't Cry (Andrew's Song), cowritten by Mandisa, Cindy Morgan, and Cathy Lee Gravitt.

5. Jerry Bridges, *The Discipline of Grace* (NavPress, 2018).

6. "Lord, I Need You" written by Matt Maher, Daniel Carson, Jesse Reeves, Kristian Paul Stanfill, and Christy L. Nockels and sung by Matt Maher.

7. Henry C. Thiessen, *Lectures in Systematic Theology* (Eerdmans, 2006).

8. "Suicide Statistics," American Foundation for Suicide Prevention, accessed December 15, 2024, https://afsp.org/suicide-statistics.